CORPUS PALLADIANUM

VOLUME III

CENTRO INTERNAZIONALE DI STUDI DI ARCHITETTURA
« ANDREA PALLADIO »

BOARD OF ADVISORS

CORPUS PALLADIANUM

Already published:

   I   THE ROTONDA, by Camillo Semenzato
  II   THE BASILICA, by Franco Barbieri
 III   THE CHIESA DEL REDENTORE, by Wladimir Timofiewitsch

In course of publication:

 IV   THE LOGGIA DEL CAPITANIATO, by Arnaldo Venditti
  V   THE VILLA EMO AT FANZOLO, by Giampaolo Bordignon Favero
 VI   THE CONVENTO DELLA CARITÀ, by Elena Bassi

In preparation:

THE CHURCH OF SAN GIORGIO MAGGIORE, by Ferdinando Forlati and Nicola Ivanoff
THE PALAZZO ANTONINI IN UDINE, by Camillo Semenzato
THE PALAZZO BARBARAN DA PORTO, by Manfredo Tafuri
THE PALAZZO CHIERICATI, by Franco Barbieri
THE PALAZZO DA PORTO FESTA IN VICENZA, by Erik Forssman
THE PALAZZO THIENE IN VICENZA, by Renato Cevese
THE PALAZZO VALMARANA-BRAGA, by Nino Carboneri
THE VILLA BADOER AT FRATTA POLESINE, by Lionello Puppi
THE VILLA BARBARO VOLPI AT MASER, by Giuseppe Mazzariol
THE VILLA CORNARO AT PIOMBINO DESE, by Douglas Lewis
THE VILLA MALCONTENTA AT MIRA, by Licisco Magagnato
THE VILLA PISANI AT BAGNOLO, by Marco Rosci
THE VILLA PISANI AT MONTAGNANA, by Francesco Cessi
THE VILLA SAREGO AT SANTA SOFIA DI PEDEMONTE, by Pietro Gazzola
THE TEATRO OLIMPICO, by Licisco Magagnato

Editor of the Series: Renato Cevese
Assistant Editor: Abelardo Cappelletti

THE REDENTORE

Wladimir Timofiewitsch

THE CHIESA DEL REDENTORE

CORPUS PALLADIANUM

VOLUME III

THE PENNSYLVANIA STATE UNIVERSITY PRESS

UNIVERSITY PARK & LONDON

GILDA D'AGARO, in collaboration with Maria Tarlà and Mario Tomasutti, executed the scale drawings of the Basilica, the Redentore, and the Rotonda and, with the collaboration of Pietro Pelzel, those of the Malcontenta and the Convento della Carità. Andrzej Pereswiet-Sołtan, under the direction of Mario Zocconi, executed the drawings for the Villa Badoera, the Loggia Bernarda, the Palazzo Barbaran Da Porto Festa, the Villa Godi Malinverni, the Villa Pisani at Bagnolo, the Villa Pisani at Montagnana, the Villa Pojana, and the Teatro Olimpico. Mario Zocconi provided those of the Palazzo Antonini and the Villa Emo, the latter in collaboration with Andrzej Pereswiet-Sołtan.

The preparation of the monographs of the Corpus Palladianum has been made possible with the aid of the CONSIGLIO NAZIONALE DELLE RICERCHE of Italy and of the ENTI FONDATORI of the Centro Internazionale di Studi di Architettura " Andrea Palladio " in Vicenza.

CONTENTS

Historical Background 13

The Plan of the Church 19

The Elevation of the Nave 21

The Elevation of the Presbytery 25

The Monks' Choir 30

The Exterior of the Church 31

The Interior Space as Related to the Votive Procession 39

The Genesis of the Design 40

Notes 49

Appendix I 53

Notes 56

Appendix II 61

Notes 63

Appendix III 65

Notes 70

Bibliography 71

Index of Persons and Places 73

List of Illustrations in the Text 75

List of Plates 77

List of Scale Drawings 79

THE CHIESA DEL REDENTORE

I - ANDREA PALLADIO, *Chiesa del Redentore, front elevation.* From *Architettura di Andrea Palladio ... con le osservazioni dell'architetto N.N.,* Vol. IV, Venice, 1743

Historical Background

The votive church of the Redentore,[1] dedicated to the Saviour during the terrible plague that devastated Venice between 1575 and 1577, is the second large sacred edifice built by Andrea Palladio in the city of the lagoons (Plate 1). Numerous sources allow us to follow with considerable exactness the history of its construction, which took place during the relatively brief period between 1577 and 1592.[2]

On September 4, 1576, the Venetian Senate discussed at length the offer of a "Mansueto francese" who claimed to have "un secretto mirabilissimo" through which "la città sarebbe stata liberata da cossj orribil mal"[3] and decided by eighty-four votes to two (with one abstention) to enter into a vow committing the Republic to build a new church "intitolata al Redentor Nostro." The vow was not limited to the construction of the church, but promised as well that "ogn'anno nel giorno che questa città sarà publicata libera dal presente contagio, sua Serenità et li successori suoi andera solennemente a visitar la predetta chiesa, a perpetua memoria del beneficio ricevuto."[4]

With the same decree of September 4th the Senate also established the ceremonies that were to precede the official announcement of the vow and made various practical arrangements for the erection of the church. These arrangements included the designation of two senators as administrative directors of the undertaking and the determination of the cost, fixed at 10,000 ducats.

The vow was officially proclaimed on September 8th by the doge, Alvise Mocenigo, before the beginning of Mass in St. Mark's. In his discourse the doge compared the circumstances that had moved the Senate to make the vow with the punishment imposed on the people of Israel after David's census, which took the form of a plague lasting three days and ended with the erection of a new altar.[5]

On September 18th of the same year two patricians were designated "Proveditori sopra la fabricha" and were immediately charged to find a location suitable for the building.[6] Of the three possible sites they presented, the Senate chose the one on the Giudecca on November 22, 1576, and at the same time arranged to buy a plot of land overlooking the canal, measuring 16 paces in length and 40 paces in depth and costing 3,000 ducats. The care of the church and the responsibility for the services were to be entrusted to the Capuchin monks living rather humbly near the area selected.[7]

At first glance, it seems rather strange that the Senate chose the costliest of all the proposed solutions. In addition to the Giudecca site, a plot in the neighborhood of San Vitale (almost in front of the present-day Accademia) costing 2,500 ducats, and a piece of land offered by the Poor Clares of Santa Croce were also under consideration.[8] The nuns put at the Senate's disposal, "senza precio alcuno," the land on which a part of their church — by that time in ruins — was located, as well as whatever construction material might be obtained in the course of demolishing the collapsing building.[9] The idea of having in their care the votive church of the Republic particularly attracted them, and in their petitions addressed to the Signoria they ardently urged this solution, attempting to anticipate all possible objections. The opinions of the "maggior Schola di theologi et canonisti" which at that time was to be found in Venice, according to the statement of the sisters, were of the same tenor. These "theologi et canonisti" evidently had to support the arguments advanced by the sisters.[10]

Detailed examination of the affair helps to explain — at least up to a certain point — the reasons that impelled the Senate to choose the most expensive land. The main cause lay in the fact that, because of the outlying position of the island, the Giudecca offered from every point of view the site most adapted to a votive temple. The numerous Italian churches erected for liberation from the plague — for example, Santa Maria della Consolazione at Todi and the Monte Berico sanctuary in Vicenza — confirm the custom of building edifices of that nature beyond the city walls. Moreover, if we consider that choosing the less costly San Vitale site would also have measurably facilitated the progress of the procession to be held there annually, we must assume that the selection of the Giudecca (which the nuns of Santa Croce in their first petition defined as "fuori et lontana") was held to be a particularly propitious one. In that location the church would also have been visible from the center of the city, which would not have been possible if it had risen in either of the other two locations under consideration.

Furthermore, the proximity of the site to the Church of Santa Croce della Giudecca probably represented a positive factor in the Senate's decision. In the nuns' second petition, as well as in the opinion of the "Schola dei theologi," the "mistero della Croce in questo flagello della peste" was alluded to with particular insistence.

The anonymous writer of this petition attempts through a series of ably-assembled arguments to demonstrate the singular advantage that would come to the Republic's votive church if it were erected on the same site as that of a house of God which preserved relics of the Cross — i.e., the site where the church of the Poor Clares of Santa Croce was located. This argument was linked to the story of David's altar, erected in the place where Solomon's temple, "che era figura come dicono li Sancti della Sanctissima Croce," probably was later built. The writer emphasized the mystical significance of the Tau symbol and ended with a reference to the exaltation of the Cross by the emperor Heraclius.

However, reconstructing a church did not in the eyes of the Signoria satisfy the meaning and importance of the vow, since an edifice remade in its original location could not be thought of as a new building; also, the nuns' gratuitous offer did not accord with the spirit of the vow, as is particularly evident when we think of the meaning inherent in the Biblical story mentioned during the proclamation of the Republic's vow.[11] Nevertheless, the nuns' subtle arguments concerning the significance that the symbol of the Cross would assume for a votive church evidently must have made an impression on the senators, as is revealed in the selection of the day for laying the first stone ("essendo quel giorno dell'inventione della Santissima Croce del Redentor nostro") and in the celebration of a Mass in the Church of Santa

Croce della Giudecca to initiate the ceremony.[12]

The nuns' petitions afford us an idea of the scrupulous examination given to the sites under consideration. The nuns who wrote them tell us, among other things, that by order of the *provveditori* the architect Rusconi visited the convent to sketch a plan of the future church on the site.[13] This means that the *provveditori* had called in experts from the very beginning; from this fact we can deduce that all of the sites under consideration were able to accommodate a building of some size, and that designs had also been executed for the other two sites, as was done in the case of Santa Croce. Supporting the latter supposition is the fact that in the Senate's deliberation of November 22nd the dimensions of the area necessary to accommodate the church were already cited.

It is difficult today to know whether the "plan" mentioned by the nuns was actually precise and more or less elaborated, or whether it was a simple sketch which — taking account of topographical conditions — merely examined the possibilities of the proposed site. The repeated citation of the "sopradetto Modello" would, however, testify in favor of the first hypothesis, and this is confirmed by several passages in the Senate's deliberations. In the decree of September 18, 1576, it is stated (among other things) that the *provveditori* had to communicate to the Signoria "in termine de giorni Tre prossimi ... tutti li luoghi che haveranno veduti";[14] it is therefore possible that the period of time which elapsed between that date and the definitive choice of the site during the second half of November was occupied in the examination of the advantages offered by the various sites under discussion.[15] The reply of the "Compagnia del Giesù" to the Signoria, wherein the Jesuits declared themselves ready to take on the responsibility of the care of the church in the event "che se ne deliberasse per il pubblico di far la chiesa votiva sul Campo Santo Vitale,"[16] strengthens the conviction that preliminary ideas had been worked out for all three of the possible solutions.

In the minutes of the meeting of November 17th, in which the sites next to the convent of the Poor Clares and in Campo San Vitale were definitely discarded, we read that in case of an eventual choice in favor of the San Vitale site the construction of a residence for the Brothers of the Society of Jesus was anticipated;[17] however, it was quickly emphasized that such a plan would not influence in the slightest the form which had been determined for the church. It is therefore legitimate to deduce that by that time there were already various plans concerning the "forma del predeto tempio" on hand, from which the Senators could make a choice. This is confirmed by the *oselle* minted in the same year of 1576, on the reverses of which are reproduced sacred buildings of various types.[18]

On February 9, 1577 (1576 according to the Venetian calculation), after a violent debate, the "forma" of the votive church was decided. The text of the decree makes it clear that the Senators were not to discuss simply the general aspect of the proposed building but were to choose a well-determined plan; this may be deduced from the concluding sentence directed to the *provveditori*, in which it is said that they were to "far principiar essa chiesa in forma quadrangular, sicome meglio parera alla maggior parte del Collegio. ..."[19]

The formulation of the sentence shows that a fully developed plan existed, by means of which the construction of the fabric could begin. The objection of Marc' Antonio Barbaro, who declared himself

II - ANDREA PALLADIO, *Chiesa del Redentore, front elevation.* From *Le Fabbriche e i Disegni di Andrea Palladio raccolti e illustrati da Ottavio Bertotti Scamozzi*, Vol. IV, Vicenza, 1783

opposed to the " forma quadrangular" and proposed instead a "forma rotonda," reveals the existence of a second, differently-shaped plan in competition with the first. The fact that exactly a week after the Senate's decision a "dissegno formato dal fedel nostro Andrea Palladio in forma quadrangulare" was registered in the "Collegio" as already approved for execution again confirms that on February 9th the Senate did not simply discuss the question of beginning, but instead adopted a fully formulated plan. In fact, the brief interval of seven days would have been insufficient for the complete articulation of a complex architectural idea; therefore the project must have undoubtedly been complete. The text of its registration, in which it is stated that "sopra esso fatto veder, che per i calcali diligentemente fatti dal detto Palladio, et dal fedel Antonio dal Ponte proto, non si spenderà nella fabricà più de ducati dodecimille dei danari della Signoria," testifies to that.[20]

The design was thus examined (as appears from the sentence quoted above) by the official assessor of the "Magistrato al Sal," Antonio Da Ponte, in order to check the accuracy of the specifications.[21] The days that elapsed between the Senate's decision and the registration of the project would have been sufficient for this official verification. In all likelihood, the plan was worked out in detail at an earlier period (between November 22 and February 19), which might provide a logical explanation of the relatively long time that elapsed between the two sittings that decided upon the erection of the votive church.[22]

During the same period in which Palladio's project was registered in the "Collegio" another strip of land 4 paces wide and 40 paces long was acquired, in addition to the land already purchased on the Giudecca. The Senate justified the additional purchase by stating that "con questo ag-

gionta" they conferred "la debita portione alla detta chiesa et alle stradelle d'intorno."[23]

Between the approval of the Palladian project and the laying of the first stone — which took place May 3, 1577 — the model of the new structure was probably executed. During the debate of February 9th, Zorzi Contarini offered a conciliatory proposal that "doi modelli de rilievo" be made, one "in forma rotonda e l'altro in forma quadrangolare con tutti gli adornamenti," indicating that up to that time no three-dimensional model of the future church existed. (In the case of buildings of large dimensions, a model was usually made only after the project had been selected.[24]) A painting formerly in the Mocenigo-Robilant collection[25] may indicate the existence of a model for the Redentore (Fig. XVII, p. 57). At the center of the painting the doge Alvise Mocenigo is portrayed with the four procurators of St. Mark's.[26] In front of him, in the upper left corner, Christ appears on a cloud, and the doge points to a model of the votive church in the lower left corner. Behind the model is a page holding a tray of coins, perhaps an allusion to the contribution of the doge, who during the Senate's sitting of November 22, 1576, personally donated 500 ducats for the erection of the church.[27] On the left appears the embankment of the Giudecca, toward which two boats loaded with construction materials are headed.

After the acquisition of another strip of land on February 17, 1577, the rectangle destined for the new edifice measured 20 paces along the shore and 40 paces in depth, for a total of 34.7 by 69.5 meters. The actual complex occupies an area of 34.8 by 71.8 meters, excluding the steps in front of the façade, which extend for another 10 meters (Scale Drawing d).

In a petition of July 21, 1581, directed

to the Signoria by the Capuchins in order to obtain a further increase to the allocation for their monastery,[28] the friars cite an area "di passa 200 in quadri" ceded by them for the erection of the church; this confirms that the building when constructed occupied a larger (i.e., deeper) area than had been foreseen. Responding to the petition, the *provveditori* explained that the extra piece of land was necessary to allow for the creation of a space in front of the church. This indicates that the preëxisting area 20 paces wide and 40 paces deep had been extended another 10 paces, and that the structure — originally envisaged as almost on the edge of the embankment — was moved back a bit.

Today the piazzetta in front of the church is about 23 meters deep, 10 meters of which are taken up by the flight of steps. If the 5 or 6 meters of the width of the street along the Giudecca — which is already evident in de' Barbari's plan — are removed from the total length of the piazzetta, the remainder would measure 17 or 18 meters, which corresponds almost exactly to the paces (17.38 meters) that the Capuchins made available. On May 27, 1577, the Capuchins bought a site for the construction of a new monastery; the plot extended immediately behind the area acquired by the Republic to the shore of the lagoon.[29] Consequently, the ceding of the 200 paces of land must have taken place only after the laying of the first stone of the church. The land acquired by the friars extended behind the land meant for the church, while the piazzetta was added in front of it; thus it can be maintained that originally — or at least up until the time the building was begun — a piazza was not envisaged in front of the church.

It seems also that the appropriations for the construction had been taxed by unexpected expenses that occurred in the course of the work. The expenditure for the future church had been established at 10,000 ducats.[30] The text of the decree concerning the definitive form of the structure emphasizes that "oltre il fondo[31] et li donativi fatti[32] più de ducati dieci, fin dodeci mille di danari della Signoria" could not be spent, and in the registration of the project it was again repeated that — according to an inspection of the design — the cost of the construction would not be over 12,000 ducats. However, as early as July 23, 1579, the *provveditori* declared that they did not have any funds to continue the work.[33] On November 6th of the same year they discussed these material difficulties at length,[34] and it was made clear on that occasion that, in order to maintain "la forma e la grandezza" decided by the "Autorità del Consiglio,"[35] the sum allotted would not have been sufficient in any case for the completion of the work. Up until the consecration of the church, which took place September 27, 1592, another 78,100 ducats drawn from public funds were added to the initial 12,000 ducats. Even considering that the first amount had been estimated simply for the rough construction of the building (as may be deduced from the tenor of the decree of September 14, 1576), the difference between the sum envisaged and what was actually spent is so remarkable that it cannot be explained as a simple error of calculation.

On July 13, 1577, the Senate had arranged a "pubblicar sana, et libera da contagio essa Città,"[36] and in the same sitting it was established that a procession to the votive church should be held every year on the third Sunday in July. The first procession — the first "Festa del Redentore" — took place on the 21st of the same month.[37] On September 27, 1592, fifteen years later, the patriarch Lorenzo Priuli solemnly consecrated the church.[38]

a) The Chiesa del Redentore seen from the Zattere

THE PLAN OF THE CHURCH

In a letter presumed to be by Palladio written to Count Capra, we read that the votive church had been planned "a croce latina."[39] However, the form of this plan does not correspond to the plan of the actual building (Scale Drawing *a*; Figs. V, VI, pp. 24-25). The character of the structure is determined by only one of its axes, the longitudinal one. The church is composed of autonomous spatial units which follow one another along a single axis, which is anticipated on the exterior by the ample flight of stairs. The first spatial unit inside is the rectangle of the nave, flanked on the sides by chapels; it is separated from the next unit by the quite perceptible turn of the walls at its end, which emphatically separates the rectangular unit of the nave from the next space, the crossing with its trefoil plan. The principal apse of this second spatial unit is formed by a semicircular colonnade behind the main altar; it places the centralized space in communication with the rectangular monks' choir, which is arranged along the same longitudinal axis. Its slightly concave back wall emphasizes once again the preëminent importance of the continuous longitudinal axis. None of these three successive spatial units has the width necessary to act as a counter to the long axis or to suggest a transverse axis within the whole complex relative to the prevalent longitudinal course. Each in itself, however, contains a transverse axis, and thus each individual element nearly assumes an independent position in respect to the others.

These preliminary observations are meant to show that the plan of the Redentore must not be understood as that of a true cross construction — i.e., a structure created by a longitudinal and a transverse body — but simply as a series of connected spaces. The first, that of the nave, is formed by a rectangle whose width is almost exactly in a 1:2 relationship to its length; along its long sides are three chapels, each placed parallel to the principal axis. The lesser sides of the rectangles of the chapels project into small apses (Scale Drawings *f*, *g*; Fig. X, p. 37), which have short passages linking the chapels. From the third chapel — counting from the entrance — the passages on both sides of the nave open into corridors which, turning round the two lateral apses, connect the chapels with the two sacristies flanking the presbytery apse.

In the articulation of the spatial shell, the nave and presbytery are in close relationship. The piers along the nave have coupled half-columns attached to them, defining the outer surfaces of the wall. This motif is repeated in the beveled crossing piers in the second spatial unit of the church.

Subtle adjustments like the considerable narrowing of the walls between nave and crossing, corresponding to the triumphal arch and the change in level of the pavement, separate the two areas and at the same time assure that each has full spatial autonomy. The corners of the nave form a right angle; thus the space appears to be defined and concluded. The crossing piers, however, are arranged diagonally, although their attached half-columns are placed in relation to an ideal square plan under the dome. This arrangement seems in a certain sense to restrain the square space from opening out into the adjacent spaces. Thus the nave and presbytery are conceived as self-sufficient spatial units, but at the points where they meet one wall section is structurally bonded to the other, and they seem to grow together.

The side chapels along the nave have a special character due to their expansion into apses and their articulation with pilasters alone. They are subordinate to the central space and assume, at least in plan,

III - ANDREA PALLADIO, *Chiesa del Redentore, transverse section*. From *Architettura di Andrea Palladio ...
con le osservazioni dell'architetto N.N.*, Vol. IV, Venice, 1743

the position of spaces complementary to the axis of the longitudinal area (Scale Drawings *a*, *f*).

The lateral apses in the crossing are parts of a trichotomous group culminating in the apse of the main altar. The spaces here are broad, and the area under the dome remains quite distinct from the lateral apses and equally distinct from the apse of the main altar; the lateral apses are articulated by great pilasters and that of the altar by the transparent screen of columns. Autonomy and interdependence are as perceptible here as was the case in the relationship between the side chapels and the central nave, while a preëminent position is reserved to the apse of the main altar.

The essential character of the configuration of this plan is therefore given by the sequence of spaces differentiated among themselves; one is a centralized space made up of various elements; the other is the rectangular nave, the longitudinal axis of which culminates in the special articulation of the main apse. The colonnade which defines the principal apse does not suggest an opening into the adjacent area placed at the conclusion of the longitudinal axis, since the apse is tightly bound by the trichotomous division; the structural division between the apse and the monks' choir is the semicircle of columns; and the monks' choir thus forms a subordinate and essentially separate space devoted to practical purposes.

The Elevation of the Nave

The giant Corinthian half-columns transform the walls of the nave into a series of four narrow bays alternating with three wide bays; great, round arches in the wide bays open into the chapels (Figs. IV, p. 23, and IX, pp. 32-33; Scale Drawing *d*). These arches, supported on the Corinthian

pilasters of the minor order, are linked to the entablature above by means of volutes (Plates 26, 27); the wall surfaces between the half-columns of the narrow bays are hollowed out into two niches, one above the other, separated by a horizontal rectangle let into the wall.[40] The statues meant for these niches were never made.[41] A certain effort is necessary on the part of the observer in order not to falsify the relationship of these empty, unframed niches to the rest of the elevation and to be able instead to imagine them as adorned with the missing statues (Figs. IX, pp. 32-33, and X, p. 37).[41]

The elevation's articulation is given additional clarity by its horizontal subdivision. Under the entablature three zones can be distinguished: the lowest one begins at the socle and is concluded by a strip of meander ornament (Plate 53); the median zone continues on up to the entablature of the minor order; the upper zone runs from there up through the entablature of the giant order.

Turning to the side chapels (Plates 28, 29), we note the continuation of the meander band and of the minor entablature from which the barrel vault springs. By maintaining the same horizontal scheme and by holding the levels consistent in both the nave and in the chapels, the spatial coherence of the interior has been maintained. In a careful examination, we find that the piers along the nave and the openings into the chapels are practically equal in length; the difference, in fact, is only a few centimeters. The deep recesses of the chapels might be defined as the "negative" parts of the spatial envelope, in opposition to the " positive " parts represented by the piers, which alternate with the chapels down the sides of the nave.

The columns of the giant order, united by the powerful entablature, seem almost to form the first perimeter of the space, like a screen placed in front of massive structural walls. While it is theoretically sustainable, this interpretation does not actually correspond to the visual impression. Between the giant half-columns the eye first perceives a rhythmical alternation of wider and narrower bays, made up of chapel openings and slices of wall (Plates 22, 24). In the narrow wall surfaces between the half-columns various architectonic motifs are crowded together; the niches (to be imagined as containing statues) are proportioned vertically, the upper ones rising into the zone of the capitals of the giant order and both upper and lower ones having only a narrow area between their edges and the adjacent columns. Ornamental reliefs interlaced with crosses of the consecration are inserted between the lower niches and the architrave of the minor order.

The sober articulation, the large, calm forms of the altars, the thermal windows, and the compactness of the barrel vaults allow the side chapels to emerge without strong plastic articulation. Thus we are struck by the rhythmic alternation between the narrow, vibrant bays along the nave and the wide, deep concavities of the chapels.

At this point we must question whether it is legitimate to remove the half-columns from their context as structural elements belonging to a complete order, in order to emphasize instead the role they play in relation to the wall surfaces. Behind the unfluted half-columns, the walls — as has already been noted — represent the plane of the continuous wall surface, which forms a spatial shell for the nave. This surface, however, loses its compactness and largely dissolves between the coupled half-columns; in fact, the bare niches should not be considered simply as cavities recessed in the walls in which shadows collect; instead, one must imagine them to be dimly defined and a little vague, containing a continuous

and symbolic interplay of statues which would cause the mass of the wall to dissolve itself optically across the surface. A fully rounded half-column is in itself a form with an undulating movement, and thus there is all the more reason that the half-column in the Redentore — especially when it appears against a smooth wall — assumes the character of a high relief emerging from an imprecisely defined background. In this way the gigantic half-columns effectively free themselves from any tight relationship to the entablature and assume — together with the walls between them, which are almost dissolved by the concavities of the niches — the character of bays of monumental plasticity.

If we keep in mind that these bays of high relief are also the piers of the nave wall, and that together with the side chapels they articulate the space in a measured rhythm, it will then be clear that this rhythmical progression and the modulation of space occur only along the surfaces of the immediate enclosure of the principal space. It is thus not the half-columns which define the limits of the principal space, but the surfaces of the piers—and these seem almost irrelevant to the structure behind. In the corners of the rectangular nave the same motifs are echoed (Plates 23, 33) — without, however, having the surface plasticity of the piers between the chapels — which combined form the unitary structure of the spatial body.

The nave is covered by a barrel vault without articulation (Fig. III, p. 20; Plate 25) and is curved to correspond to the longitudinal axis; it is intersected by the lunettes of the thermal windows. The entablature largely hides the base of the vault and of the lunettes. Indeed, the interruption of the light laterally across the surface of the vault, which is itself simple and bright, makes it appear even more

IV - Andrea Palladio, *Chiesa del Redentore, longitudinal section.* From *Le Fabbriche e i Disegni di Andrea Palladio raccolti e illustrati da Ottavio Bertotti Scamozzi*, Vol. IV, Vicenza, 1783

softened in form and allows it to become the source of a diffused luminosity in the interior space.

In Palladian criticism, the height of the nave of the Redentore is judged to be too low in relation to the other two dimensions. As early as the time of Bertotti-Scamozzi, we read that the height of the space "non è regolata con nessuna delle tre medie insegnate e praticate dal nostro architetto "; [42] and the same author later reports that even measuring "con la media proporzionale armonica, che fra le tre medie è la più bassa," the height of the longitudinal body appears lower by " piedi 2 oncie 5 "—a finding which led him to postulate an " isbaglio degli Operaj."

Bertotti's calculation requires a brief critical scrutiny. In his description he gives

the following dimensions for the space: 45 *piedi* in width, 90 *piedi* in length, and 57 *piedi*, 7 *oncie* in height. With these measurements, the neoclassical scholar established that the height of the space is not well proportioned to the other two dimensions. But if the measurements of the length and width reported by Bertotti are compared with the actual measurements, we see at once that they do not coincide. The width, which he indicated as 45 *piedi* (about 15.6 meters), is actually 16.8 meters, and the length indicated as 90 *piedi* (about 31.3 meters) actually measures 33.3 meters. On the other hand, the measurement of 57 *piedi*, and 7 *oncie* (approximately 20.1 meters) is not far from the actual height of the space, which is 20.4 meters. The discrepancy may be explained

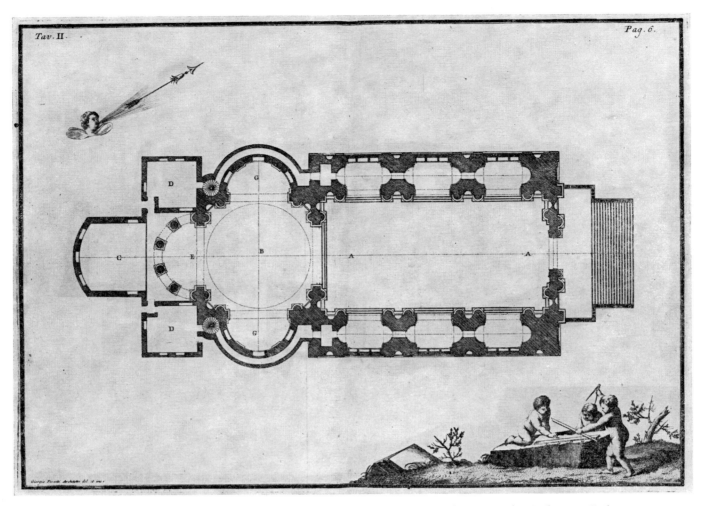

V - ANDREA PALLADIO, *Chiesa del Redentore, plan.* From *Architettura di Andrea Palladio ...*
con le osservazioni dell'architetto N.N., Vol. IV, Venice, 1743

very simply: Bertotti-Scamozzi did not cal-culate his measurements from wall to wall, but only from the outer surfaces of the socle of the giant order. A measurement taking this fact into account corresponds almost exactly to his measures, i.e., to 15.4 meters for the width and 31.6 meters for the length.

In calculating "con la media proporzio-nale armonica," Bertotti-Scamozzi proceed-ed from a relationship clearly determined by Palladio in the *Quattro Libri*. Indeed, he clearly refers to the particular sentence which states: " Si può anche ritrovare un'altezza, che sarà minore, ma non di meno proportionata."[43] This involves a numerical series determined according to the arithmetical progression of 6:9:12, in which the first number indicates the width,

the second the height, and the third the length of the space. In this case, Palladio demonstrates that even a height of 8 *piedi* "proportionata" to the other two dimen-sions could exist. The series 6:9:12 is therefore transformed into 6:8:12, ar-ranged according to the rules of harmonic proportion. The first two numbers thus form a "diatesseron" and the relationship between the second and the third is equal to a "diapente," while the two external numbers of the series are in the relation-ship of having a "diapason" between them.[44]

The height of 60 *piedi*, defined as "cor-retta" by Bertotti with the two dimensions of 45 and 90 *piedi* in proportion to it, also gives the same proportional harmonic relationship of 3:4:6. If we attempt to calculate according to the same proportions

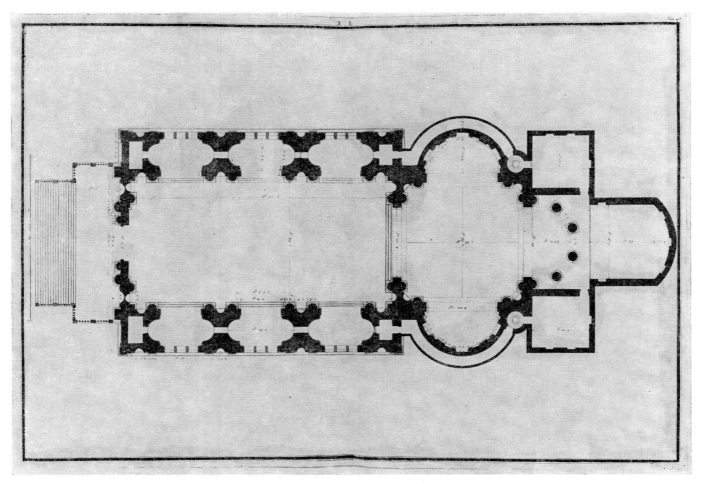

VI Andrea Palladio, *Chiesa del Redentore, plan.* From *Le Fabbriche e i Disegni di Andrea Palladio raccolti e illustrati da Ottavio Bertotti Scamozzi*, Vol. IV, Vicenza, 1783

the least height possible for the longitudinal body according to the actual measurements, we obtain a height of almost 22 meters. By this calculation the height of the actual space is not "piedi 2, oncie 5" lower than the proportional relationship; however, keeping in mind the actual length and width of the nave, it is a good meter-and-a-half lower than the height which the proportional relationships among the dimensions would allow.

These observations still do not give a satisfactory explanation of the "too low" height of the nave, and the problem will remain unsolved as long as the longitudinal body is considered in isolation. The last sentence of the chapter in the *Quattro Libri* quoted above, in which Palladio deals with the proportionate arrangement of the

height of a space, leads one to doubt the suggestion of an "isbaglio degli Operaj." Palladio concludes his explanation by writing: "Sono ancora altre altezze di volti, le quali non cascano sotto la regola e di queste si hauerà da servire l'architetto, secondo il suo giudicio, e secondo la necessità."

THE ELEVATION OF THE PRESBYTERY

Coming from the nave, we enter the space dominated by the dome by way of three steps, which constitute a caesura between the longitudinal space of the nave and the central space (Plates 33, 37; Scale Drawing *e*). The central area of this space is defined by four powerful, beveled crossing piers (Plates 36, 38), which unite with the lateral apses and with the colonnade arranged in a semicircle behind the high altar. The surface of the crossing piers presents motifs noted earlier in the piers which flank the longitudinal nave. Here, however, there is a substantial difference in the positioning of the half-columns: in the nave piers they are on the same plane as the surface between them, while here — as we can see from the base and the entablature (Plates 44, 45, 61) — they are placed against ideal walls which would correspond in plan to a square space surmounted by the dome and articulated in each corner by the half-columns. Flanking the openings which lead into the apses rise giant "colonne quadre"[45] which act as a connection between the prism under the dome and the adjacent spaces in the apses. Above the beveled surfaces of the crossing piers rise pendentives with a slight horizontal curve immediately above the entablature (Plate 43); above the half-columns and the "square columns" rise the crossing arches with their double profiles. The drum above, rising behind a balustrade made up of small, slender, bipartite balusters, is articulated by pilasters into sixteen sections (Plate 42). The sections in the diagonal axes are pierced by vertical rectangular windows, while the others each contain a narrow, shallow niche with an arched head. Above the entablature supported by the drum pilasters the stilted dome rises upward to turn into a smooth hemisphere (Plates 41, 43). The light that shines through the oculus from the lantern frees the dome from any sense of heaviness, and the luminosity coming from the center of the space does not permit its degree of curvature or its actual height to be precisely grasped. The bright surface makes the dome seem to be an organism completely free from the weight of the architectonic structure, as if it were poised in the air and made of light.

In the lateral apses, the walls (Plates 34, 35) are divided into three sections by Corinthian pilasters of a giant order, the central bay being a little wider than the lateral ones. The horizontal subdivision of the wall into three zones, one above the other — as in the nave — is repeated here. Each field of the middle and upper zones frames a vertical rectangular window. The windows of the middle zone are characterized by aedicular frames with fluted pilasters and alternately triangular and curvilinear pediments, while the windows in the upper zone have only simple cornices.

Unlike the lateral apses, the one behind the main altar has five intercolumniations, each of the same width, formed by four columns and by two half-columns, also of the giant order and Corinthian (Plates 37, 39, 40). They sustain the entablature, which continues from the crossing piers and supports the apsidal vault. Considering the difference in the number of intercolumniations of the central apse relative to that of the lateral apses, it is clear that the crossing is not simply a spatial nucleus of three shells, but is a multiple organism composed of a central prism with semicircular spaces joined to it.

The pairs of half-columns in the space beneath the dome are integrated (as earlier in the nave) with the wall surfaces of the piers, which again have niches without mouldings, to form monumental areas of high relief. Taking into account the position of the half-columns, these areas — which intrude into the space of the crossing — anticipate the projection of the crossing piers which support the arches marking the beginning of the lateral apses. Whereas in the nave one has the impression that the vault rests on the entablature of the giant order, the pendentives of the dome are formed like surfaces stretched between the double-profiled arches and the

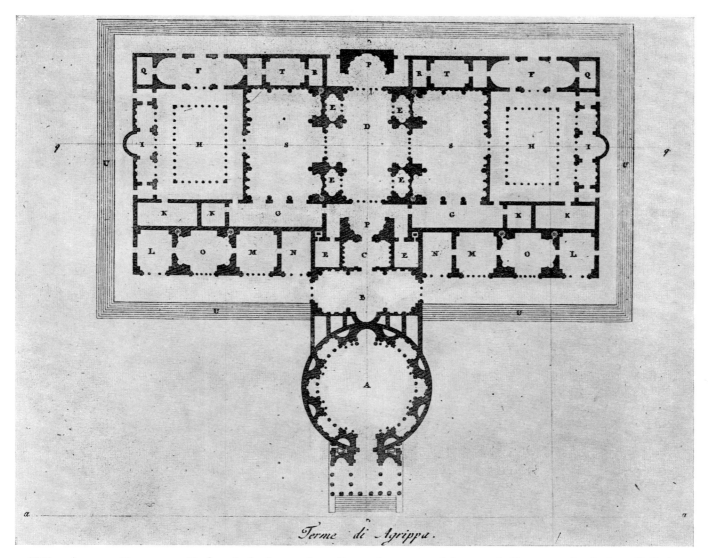

VII - ANDREA PALLADIO, *Baths of Agrippa, plan.* From *Le terme dei romani disegnate da Andrea Palladio,* by Ottavio Bertotti Scamozzi, Vicenza, 1797

base of the drum; the drum then seems to be an entablature stretched up from the pendentives to the hemisphere of the dome. When resolved in this way, the verticality of the space and the structural function of the crossing piers is not emphasized.

When a pier is not clearly emphasized as the actual supporting member for a structural system, but seems instead to be primarily an element in a wall system defining a space, the relationship between that which is truly part of the constructive system and that which is not is obscured and deëmphasized. This is the case with these crossing piers in the relationship between the supporting half-columns and the wall surfaces between them. The crossing piers are primarily monumental areas of high relief, like those in the nave, and are integrated with the ideal square space under the dome which rises up as a spatial prism, gradually resolving itself into rounded forms. The spatial prism within the crossing becomes primarily a coordinating element between the three elements making up the triconch crossing.

If we observe the articulation of the lateral apses without, for the moment, taking account of the windows, we note that because of the socle and the entablature the walls take on the aspect of continuous and undifferentiated surfaces of the body of the church, just as was earlier seen in the examination of the nave. In these space-enclosing "entities" the pilasters appear as projections of columns. Considering, however, that the degree of expressive intensity of projected columns is less than that of half-columns, one has the impression that the apses are given a lesser importance, and that they exist in a subordinate relationship to the space of the dome. These projected columns, however, suggest that their archetype is to be found elsewhere in the space.

If we were to project the apse wall back onto one side of the crossing, we would obtain on that hypothetical wall surface an articulation in which the outer bays relate to the inner bay by the ratio of 1 to 2, and whose breadth is the same as that of the wall surface of the diagonal bays. The central prism of the crossing would then be enclosed on all sides by wall surfaces which the colossal order would articulate into three equally small bays around each beveled corner of the square space, with a wider bay in-between. There is a similar system in the domed interior space of the small church of Santa Maria delle Zitelle, whose construction for the most part can be traced back to a project by Palladio.[46]

Thus considered, the apses of the Redentore are in effect substitutes for the side walls of the central prism of space in the crossing; in other words, they are not spaces in themselves, but are subordinate to the space of the dome. However, windows are inserted in the intercolumniations of the apses which by their framing and horizontal mouldings link the piers in a system recalling a two-storey façade system. If in the bays of high relief the surfaces seem to be dissolved through the niches, in the lateral apses the surfaces are resolved into a kind of structural stratification. Whereas the structures of the piers give them a vertical emphasis, the articulation of the lateral apses — notwithstanding the giant order — accentuates the horizontal progression. The piers carrying the dome give the impression of being characterized by monumental rhythmic decorative elements; on the other hand, the articulation of the lateral apses reminds one of an arrangement typical of secular façades, and this secular character is accentuated by the fact that the apses lack altars. However much the abovementioned details may contribute to giving the apses a special character, we must nevertheless note that the relationship of the successive spatial areas to the central space in the end determines their spatial significance. The apsidal walls indicate where the viewpoint of the potential observer would have to be, just as if he were standing in front of a "façade" which does not lead him into a space. If a façade is being developed on a semicircle and linked to another space, its apsidal cavity will best characterize its spatial content. The spherical vaults of the apses form such cavities; they are white and unarticulated, and they stretch rigidly from the crossing arches to the principal entablature that continues from the crossing piers around into the lateral apses. This type of vault characterizes the relationship between the apses and the central space; the articulation of the walls of the apses emphasizes the latter's autonomy in relation to the central space; and the structural framework composed of the " square columns," the arches, and the entablatures expresses and fixes the circular progression of these spaces and their subordinate position to the principal space under the dome.

The main apse is differentiated from the spatial context of the area beneath the dome and from the lateral apses by the isolated columns, which are arranged in a semicircle with five intercolumniations and thus are not comparable in their archi-

Giorgio Fossati Archi.to inc.

VIII - ANDREA PALLADIO, *Chiesa del Redentore, left flank.* From *Architettura di Andrea Palladio ... con le osservazioni dell'architetto N.N.,* Vol. IV, Venice, 1743

tectonic system to anything else in the building — the isolated columns behind the main altar naturally cannot be considered as a projection of an architectonic system upon a wall. The colonnade of the apse is a well-defined semicircle, which implies its own inherent completion into a closed circle as a spatial entity with a clearly individualized structure.

Here, too, the apse's relationship with the central space is determined by its spatial "content." A series of isolated columns can form a boundary between two spaces, and such a series of columns arranged in a semicircle can separate one space from another; but only by means of a vault can such a delimiting series of columns assume the character of a real space. The vault in question is a simple, white, unarticulated cavity, a covering that derives formal clarity only from the framework composed of the "square columns," the arch, and the entablature which runs inside. The apse of the main altar is in a preëminent position with respect to the central space, precisely because the half-columns of the crossing piers are here transformed into full columns. But its spatial content — like that of the lateral apses — is still subordinated to the nucleus beneath the dome, which is closed off and defined as a spatial entity by the monumental crossing piers and their sense of high relief.

In the longitudinal nave of the church, the sucession of vigorously outlined sections of wall with their effect of high relief defines a spatial unit, accompanied by the conjoined and, in a certain sense, autonomous spaces of the side chapels. However, in the presbytery the definition of a spatial unit by the same means is rather less evident, because the principal entablature of the giant order also runs round the conjoined spaces, and because the impression of vaulting is not as intense and evident

as in the case of the barrel vault. If it is true that the apses are structually differentiated from the central nucleus, the degree of their autonomy is less than that of the nave chapels. Moreover, the sections of wall with high relief which announce and introduce adjoining spaces do not meet at right angles in their conjunctions with the adjoining spaces, but at beveled angles. Unlike the longitudinal nave, the presbytery — notwithstanding its very clear articulation — represents an attenuation of spatial boundaries. In this spatial complex, which is both centralized and well differentiated, the conjoined units are linked (i.e., in a purely formal sense, by the semicircular ground-plan and the half-dome vault) not to the spatial prism of the central nucleus but to the dominating space created by the rotundity of the dome.

THE MONKS' CHOIR

The simplicity of the walls in the monks' choir (Plates 50, 54) is consistent with the Capuchin ideal of poverty. The fact that as early as the first year of construction the monks had expressed to the Senate their disapproval of the church's splendor — as contradicting the spirit of the Order — confirms the desire to confer a particular character to the choir in respect to the church proper.[47]

The walls of the room are devoid of any plastic articulation. The only ornaments are windows — one in each of the two lateral walls, and three in the slightly concave wall at the back — and a slender, flat band marking the springing of the low vault.

In a careful analysis, many details of the structure emerge as motifs planned to enhance the luministic effect. Five large windows, which are strongly splayed toward the inside in order to increase the flood of light, make this small space the brightest area in the whole building.[48] Three of these windows are in the wall behind the choir, on an axis with the three central inter-columniations of the exedra. This is not due, however, to practical reasons; since the back wall is slightly curved, the distance between the sources of light and the inter-columniations of the exedra is almost equal in each case. Due to a slight narrowing of the walls of the choir, the light is concentrated on the four completely round columns; thus, in relation to the entire structure, the monks' choir does not assume a concrete spatial value. From the aesthetic point of view, the choir does not represent a new space with a particular articulation, but only a point of particular intensity of light which — like the brilliant surfaces of the church proper — seems to create a luminous area behind the columns, com-prehensible only optically (Plate 22). In relation to the light that spreads under the dome (actually with equal intensity), the light of the choir produces an effect of greater intensity. The columns of the exedra, which are not directly illuminated in front, lose their plasticity against the luminous background; seen against the light they take on a linearity as if, being darker in tone, they existed on a light surface made up of the luminous space of the choir, with which they form an optical unity. The two elements, dark and light, conclude the tribune space.

It is useful to emphasize that in this case we are not concerned with a spatial " flight to infinity " or with an effect of baroque scenography. Instead, precisely at this point the centralized space that forms the predominant spatial and structur-al unit of the entire organism finds its unequivocal conclusion. This " wall of light," defined by vaguely-outlined motifs, is aesthetically analogous to any of the wall surfaces of the church, which are luminous

and white in tonality. In both cases, the effect of the enclosing structures is not determined by the contrast between the surfaces and their plastic articulation or that between the projecting and recessed elements, but by the harmony between open and closed areas and the soft *sfuma-tura* contrast between light and shadow.

THE EXTERIOR OF THE CHURCH

As we have seen in the building's in-terior, the structural subdivision of the organism into units which follow one after the other is also clearly emphasized on the outside (Scale Drawing *c*). When viewed from the side (Fig. VIII, p. 29; Plate 17), the building — which rises on a podium about 2.5 meters high — seems to be divided into individual and completely diversified parts: the longitudinal block of the nave, the vertical thrust of the presbytery, and the structure which encloses the monks' choir. The different treatment of the various surfaces emphasizes once again the particular character of each of these three parts.

An order of Corinthian pilasters — re-peating the rhythm of the interior articu-lation — articulates the lateral walls of the nave into a series of alternately wide and narrow bays. The buttresses, placed above the roof of the chapels in pairs flanking the great tripartite thermal win-dows, echo the sequence of the interior structure.

In contrast to the variously articulated walls of the nave, the high, smooth walls of the apses rise with a prominent vertical thrust. This verticality is emphasized both by the shape of the apses and by the slender, round towers placed asymmetrically behind them. The position of the towers — which is independent with respect to the rest of the structure, as the treatment

Tav. I

IX - Andrea Palladio, *Chiesa del Redentore, lor*
con le osservazioni dell'arch

Piedi 15. Vicentini

al section. From *Architettura di Andrea Palladio ...*
N.N., Vol. IV, Venice, 1743

of the line of the roof overhang plainly shows (Plate 16) — serves to intensify the effect of verticality. The articulation of the exterior of the monks' choir is limited simply to windows.

A precise view of the church's flanks from outside is possible from only a few points today; actually one can only see the side squarely rather than foreshortened from the court to the west of the church. Otherwise, a lateral view of the entire structure is obtainable only from a great distance away — for example, from the Chiesa dei Gesuati or from the Piazzetta — and it is always a little foreshortened and hidden by the houses of the Giudecca. Moreover, a distant view obviously does not permit a close examination of details, and for this reason the façade is actually the only part of the exterior which is clearly visible (Fig. I, p. 12; Plate 3).

The arrangement of the façade is determined by the structure of the internal space. The almost-square surface which defines the corresponding unit of the nave inside forms the central part of the elevation, flanked by sections corresponding to the side chapels and, above and on a slightly recessed plane, the surfaces of the first pair of buttresses (Scale Drawing b).

In the central section of the façade are two half-columns and two pilasters — or "square columns," according to Palladio[49] — of a composite order, which support a great triangular pediment. In the central intercolumniation, whose dimensions are considerably broader than those of the lateral ones, is the entrance portal, which is composed of half-columns surmounted by a triangular pediment. The other two intercolumniations have niches, framed by pilasters supporting pediments and containing statues (Plate 5).

The Corinthian pilasters which appear on the sides of the church are used also on the front to frame the lateral sections of the façade (Plate 6) which, as we have seen, are nothing other than the frontal walls of the chapels. Thus the surfaces here, as at the internal angles of the chapels, are blocked at the ends by paired pilasters. The pilasters which define the internal side of each lateral section are partly cut off from view by the "square columns" of the central part. The surfaces of the buttresses above are also faced with Istrian stone and terminated by elements resembling pilasters (Plates 8, 9).

At the level of the upper face of the podium which runs along the whole perimeter of the church a platform extends in front of the central part of the façade, reached by the wide flight of stairs leading to the entrance portal (Plate 7).[50] The treatment of these elements indicates the same organic connection between the exterior and interior of the building that has already been observed in the articulation of the rest of the exterior. The façade is not in this case a decorative wall erected in front of an architectural unit which is structurally independent of it, but is rather an external anticipation of the interior arrangement. This close connection prevented Palladio from creating an empty formal scheme, and the façade consequently acquires a character exclusive to the structure itself.[51]

This sort of connection likewise occurs in the case of the façade of San Giorgio Maggiore, which was constructed according to the same scheme of vertical tripartition. But there one has the impression that projecting columns bearing a triangular pediment are attached to the central part of a basilican façade, whereas the façade of the Redentore suggests the idea of a principal central unit with short subsidiary units joined symmetrically to its sides. The three parts of the Redentore's façade do not meld into an indivisible unity; in fact, the shafts of the pilasters which define the central part create a clear break with the two wings. The tripartition, which corresponds to the interior spatial structure, is consistent with the overall conception of the building. The façade of the Redentore is not just a surface composed of three vertical units joined together, but an organism of multiple layers made up of various parts superimposed upon one another and articulated in both height and depth (Plates 10, 11).

The architectural concept realized here is based on the progressive recession of the structural units from the prominent central unit to the lateral sections. This theme is anticipated in the two niches of the façade and in the entrance portal. The niches, in comparison to the framing of the portal, are in fact smaller and flatter than the latter, which is much larger and more strongly projecting. The slightly recessed walls of the chapels unite with the "pronaos" of the central unit to form a triad, which vitally influences the external aspect of the façade, and the surface above the principal pediment and the recessed lateral supporting walls repeat the motif. The entire façade appears to be an organism made up of numerous groups of three, but since each of these triads is composed of surfaces arranged on two different levels it becomes a play of surfaces articulated in successive planes.

As these surfaces succeed each other from bottom to top, their ascending rhythm seems to be restrained by the cornice of the hipped roof above the central section. Since its surface, slanting back from the façade, cannot be seen from nearby, the horizontal closing of the upper triad creates an unpleasant interruption of the upward progression. One thus understands the reason why the elevation, viewed from close-by (Plate 4) and cut off from the rest of the edifice, may produce an impression of "pressing down."[52] Whereas the façade

of San Giorgio Maggiore is intended to be seen from far away and across a wide expanse of water, that of the Redentore implies a different kind of viewpoint—one from the banks of the Zattere, which it faces (Plates 2, 3).[53] From that point, the alternating play of surfaces is attenuated into a relief-like effect, while the vertical progression leads beyond the roof surface and terminates in the crowning dome and two bell-towers. Here the question arises of whether or not it is correct to assume that Palladio conceived his design on the basis of a distant perspective, or even from any particular viewpoint.

In setting out the history of the church's construction, we mentioned that in 1576 the Republic had not only vowed to erect a church, but had also promised to institute a votive procession every year. The first procession took place on July 21, 1577.[54] The *libro delle cerimonie* of the Republic and a letter by an eyewitness written the following day give an account of the event. The letter, published the same year under the signature of Mutio Lumina (probably a pseudonym),[55] describes the route of the procession, which assembled all the ecclesiastical and civil dignitaries in the train of the doge and the patriarch.

The procession was able to reach the church on foot, " essendo stato fatto un ponte sopra galee, barchi, et piate, quale passava dalle colonne di San Marco fino a San Zuanne della Zudecha."[56] The church, the goal of the procession, had scarcely been begun in that year. Even though in the official description of the ceremony it is affirmed that "già è fatta buona parte della fondamenta," the work could not have progressed much in three months, as the writer of the letter himself confirms. He states clearly that "la Chiesa visitata non è quasi principiata." For that reason, a temporary construction had been erected on the site, which Lumina describes as follows: " Era fatto una porta a detta Chiesa, coperta maestrevolmente di minutissime foglie d'alberi levata da' tronconi, dentro dalla quale vi era una assai lunga strada coperta di panni fini di molto prezzo, dalla quale si giungea in un spaciodobbato di cuoi d'oro, e razzi finissimi nel so Choro acconcio gratiosamente, e admezo del quale era su per molti gradi un'altare eminente con l'imagine del Nostro Redentore...." The text of the *Cerimoniali* offers a still more exact description of the temporary part of the church, indicated in the letter as the "Choro": "...era preparato un'altare eminente, a fine che nel passar della processione le genti facessero riverentia et oratione per ditta liberatione; all'incontro del qual altare era preparato un luogo in forma di Teatro con una sedia per sua Sublimità et con banche adornate per la Serenissima Signoria et altri Senatori."

The two descriptions, which complement each other, offer a clear idea of the route of the procession and of the setting in which its last phase was completed. In order to grasp the essential nature of the Palladian structure, it is important to consider the provisional arrangement of the area intended to accommodate the final phase of the solemn celebration. The whole complex, made of wood, cloth, and leaves, may be understood in this case as a moveable frame equipped for a particular event. Within this provisional space, we can clearly distinguish the "luogo in forma di Teatro" which was the point where the procession itself ended. The abovementioned description in the *Cerimoniali* alludes, moreover, to a centrally-planned space wrapping uniformly around the altar.

Nevertheless, within a year the Senate had decided to abandon that particular route for the procession. In 1578 two bridges were constructed " per commodità della città": " l'uno a Santa Maria Zubenigo " on the Grand Canal, " et l'altro all'hospetal dello Spirito Santo " across the Giudecca canal (Fig. XXIV, p. 67).[57] The new processional route can be reconstructed with certainty by means of de' Barbari's plan and the large view of Venice executed about 1625 which was formerly in the Castello del Buonconsiglio in Trent.[58] After crossing the first bridge, the route went through the present-day Calle del Traghetto di San Gregorio to the Calle del Bastion and along the *fondamenta* (the stretch of embankment used as a street) of the Rio Fornae leading to the Zattere.

If one follows the old route today, he will be more than a little amazed. The narrow and tortuous lanes, winding through an area crowded with buildings, cut off one's view of the church — the goal of the procession — for most of the way; it does not even appear at the beginning of the *fondamenta* of the Rio Fornae. Only after drawing closer to the Zattere does one see the mass of the Redentore, rising over the low houses of the Giudecca beyond a slight curve of the canal (Plate 2). The votive church deceptively appears from that point to be a centrally-planned building: neither the lateral walls, with their paired buttresses, nor the unarticulated exterior surfaces of the apses are visible. The first thing that strikes the eye is the white marble façade which, because of its various projections, seems like a vibrant organism rather than a flat backdrop.[59] The surface of the hipped roof, invisible from nearby, at this distance gives the effect of a triangular pinnacle rising above the central section of the façade. The rising movement of each tripartite group is thus echoed by the hipped roof, the vertex of which is on a level with the impost cornice of the dome; thus, in its oblique position, the roof is interposed between the triad below and the dome above. The latter is flanked by two belltowers, forming the final and topmost

X - ANDREA PALLADIO, *Chiesa del Redentore, plan and elevation of a side chapel.*
From *Architettura di Andrea Palladio ... con le osservazioni dell'architetto N.N.*, Vol. IV, Venice, 1743

triad and concluding the impressive structural complex. The hemisphere of the dome, its slight elongation echoed by the small towers, unites with the façade of the church in a grandiose "quadro di architettura." Only a forward movement was allowed by the narrow *fondamenta* along the Rio Fornae and by the bridge across the Giudecca canal which, as Stringa notes, was placed " per diritta linea al Redentore."[60] The image of a centrally-planned edifice accompanied participants in the procession almost up until the moment they arrived at the church.

The conception of the building strengthens the hypothesis that this particular distance view had been studied for its unusual effect. The alteration of the processional route offered Palladio the possibility to present the votive church, at least on the day of the *Festa del Redentore*, as a type of celebratory construction associated with Renaissance architectural tradition. The church does not appear simply as a votive building constructed for the concluding ceremony of a rite, which could be placed in any sort of location, but as a structural organism closely linked to the procession in question and influencing the route that finished in the building itself.

Certain peculiarities of the structure which hardly have been noticed until now contribute to the monumental effect of the building's exterior. The stratified arrangement of the various planes of the elevation, calculated to be viewed from a distance, is a significant element in the dynamic rising thrust which visually unites the façade with the dome flanked by its bell-towers. The same structural concept also determines the placing of the hipped roof over the central part of the façade. If the nave had been covered with a saddleback roof like that of San Giorgio Maggiore, the impost cornice of the dome would have been blocked by its ridge in a distance view, which would have considerably disturbed the vertical effect of the elevation. A similar effort to achieve a unified overall effect is evident in the slight diminution in the height of the order in the façade's central section. Although the lower diameter of the half-column measures 1.4 meters, the columns are not 14 meters in height (i.e., 10 modules) as might be expected, but are only 13.5 meters. In order to maintain the height fixed for the composite order by Palladio in his treatise,[61] the central pediment would have had to block the cornice of the section behind, thus breaking the ideal connection between the triad of the façade and the elements above.

The slight elongation of the dome — as well as its slender, round shape and the symmetrical arrangement of the small bell-towers — can be explained in the same manner. The towers are symmetrically placed at either side of the tall hemisphere, as one alone would have spoiled the church's appearance as a centrally-planned structure. They are closely related to the dome in order to create a triadic grouping. A triad with a vertical emphasis was necessary to provide an appropriate conclusion to the ascending verticality of the façade; this was achieved by raising the dome a bit above the adjacent bell-towers which, because they are so closely related to the dome, were also required to be circular in plan.

The lack of any sort of plastic articulation on the exterior of the lateral apses perhaps may also be explained by the fact that they do not appear in a frontal view of the chuch. All this suggests that the conception of the exterior decisively influenced the much-discussed height of the interior longitudinal spaces. If the "correct" proportion of the height of the nave — calculated from the proper relationship between the width and depth of the space, according to Bertotti-Scamozzi — had been maintained, it would have considerably altered the façade of the building. A clear example supporting this hypothesis is offered by Giorgio Massari's Chiesa dei Gesuati on the Zattere, located almost directly opposite the Redentore. A seventeenth-century structure inspired by the Redentore, its ensemble of dome and two bell-towers situated above the choir is almost cut in half by the roof of the high nave.

On the other hand, the slightly lowered height of the Redentore's nave not only ensures an harmonious view of the exterior elevation, but also emphasizes the axial direction and the longitudinal character of the space in the interior. It is useful in this connection to recall once again Palladio's idea that, insofar as the height of a space is concerned, each architect must proceed not simply in accordance with whatever proportional relationships he holds valid but also "secondo il suo giudicio et secondo la necessità."

The Interior Space as Related to the Votive Procession

Even a rapid study of the descriptions of the first procession is sufficient to indicate that the interior space of the Redentore must be understood as an architectural framework necessary for the final phase of the annual votive procession. These descriptions are very useful for understanding the church's internal arrangement.

The temporary structure mentioned above provided a longitudinal space which the procession traversed as if passing along an " assai lunga strada " in order to reach a " luogo in forma di Teatro " in front of which it halted; here, before an altar, the solemn ceremony was performed.

Such an arrangement corresponds to the spatial structure of the existing church, i.e., to the longitudinal nave with " festively" decorated walls followed by a centralized space. Only thus can the significance of the variety in articulation of the centermost unit be explained. The lateral apses, which lack altars, are articulated with architectonic motifs recalling secular façades; they form the space reserved for the doge and for the dignitaries of the Republic who assisted annually at the thanksgiving function.[62] The main apse, emphasized and isolated as a sacred enclosure by the motif of the columns, functionally corresponds to the main altar, which is not simply intended for the celebration of the Mass but also constitutes the objective of the procession. The architectonic structure thus expresses conceptually the Redentore's function as a votive and processional church.[63]

The building must also be considered from another point of view. Mutio Lumina reports that during the first celebration an image "del Nostro Redentore" had been placed on the temporary altar. Today, Girolamo Campagna's bronze crucifix, made about 1590 (Plate 56), is placed on the main altar. At either side, in attitudes of intercession, are statues of St. Francis, patron saint of the Order entrusted with the care of the church (Plate 60), and St. Mark, patron saint of the Republic of Venice (Plate 59). The presence of a monumental crucified Christ, in an attitude of deep suffering, was related to the plague. The contemporary sources mentioned earlier confirm that the veneration of the Cross had been a dominant concept in the church's construction.[64] If, therefore, the still-vivid memory of the plague determined from the start the decision to place a Crucifixion on the main altar, then the votive processions must not be considered merely as a ceremony of thanksgiving to

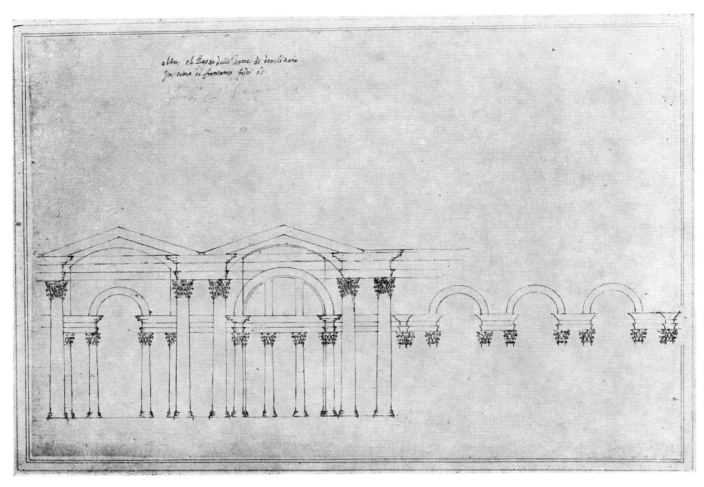

XI - ANDREA PALLADIO, *Baths of Diocletian, detail of elevation.* London, R.I.B.A., V/6

Christ the Redeemer; in remembrance of the epidemic, it commemorated in a special way the redemption of man through Christ's death on the Cross. Thus the commemorative purpose, which is the inspiration of all votive churches, also underlies the fundamental structural motif of the Redentore.

THE GENESIS OF THE DESIGN

Although the idea behind the Redentore's spatial arrangement refers to the contemporary Renaissance architectural type of sacred building created by joining a central unit to a longitudinal one, the immediate suggestions for the formulation of the theme are not found in Cinquecento architecture but in the structure of Roman thermal complexes.[65] Numerous autograph drawings by Palladio confirm the extraordinary importance that his study of these monuments assumed in the conception of the Redentore (Fig. VII, p. 27).[66] Along the central axis of all these plans are grouped large spatial units of various shapes, connected so that their perimeters seem to interpenetrate almost as if they grow into each other. Apparently the median axis of a Roman bath with its individual, autonomous spaces inspired the organization of the Redentore's plan. Not only the general conception but also many obvious formal motifs — especially in the plan of the nave — present an astonishing resemblance to Roman thermal architecture. The shape of the side chapels, the succession of spaces of equal size symmetrically arranged at each side of the

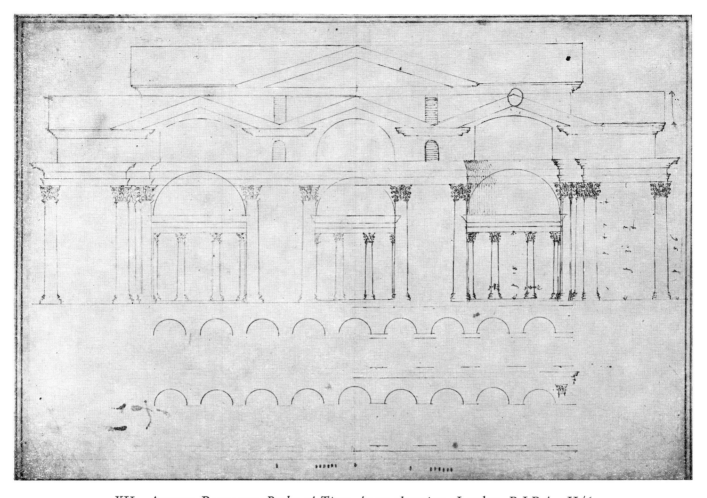

XII - ANDREA PALLADIO, *Baths of Titus, front elevation.* London, R.I.B.A., II/6

principal axis, and spatial definitions determined by the use of colonnades are
often found in Palladio's drawings.

If we compare the plan of the Redentore with those of Renaissance structures
of the same type, we note how examples
from the Early Renaissance actually display
a closer relationship to Palladio's concept
than works which are chronologically closer
to it. The Church of the Gesù in Rome,
begun about ten years earlier and hailed
as the "perfect realization"[67] of the fusion
of spaces in a single spatial shell, can be
defined as stylistically more advanced. The
substantial difference between the Renaissance type of church plan with two principal spaces and Palladio's design consists
in the different conception of the organism's
spatial structure. Whereas in the former
type the problem was to fuse two spaces

of different shapes into a unified organism,
at the source of the Palladian plan is the
desire, inspired by thermal architecture, to
create a succession of different spaces along
the same axis.

Moreover, Palladio's drawings of Roman
baths exhibit numerous formal similarities
to individual shapes and motifs of the Redentore's nave.[68] A study of the elevation
of the Baths of Diocletian (Fig. XI, p. 40),
showing the use of two orders of different
heights, is interesting in this respect.[69] If
we try to establish connections with Cinquecento architecture in order to seek ideas
which might have been stimulating to Palladio, we must conclude that a convincing
precedent for the articulation of the spatial
shell of the Redentore exists only in the
so-called plan by Raphael for St. Peter's
(Fig. XIII, p. 45). There, in fact, the

motif of surfaces which are defined by vertical elements and contain inserted niches is carried from the beveled crossing piers to the wall piers of the longitudinal nave, and then at right angles onto the entrance wall.

This type of arrangement, however, was remarkably modified by Palladio. In the Redentore, the width of the frontal surface of the piers along the nave is in an approximately 1 to 1 relationship with the openings of the side chapels; in Raphael's plan, on the other hand, the width of the piers is in an almost 1 to 2 relationship with the arched openings. In all of the thermal chambers with lateral subdivisions which Palladio drew, the piers are shown as short stretches of wall between imposing arched openings, with a giant column usually attached to the wall surfaces between the great arched openings. In certain rare drawings (Fig. XV, p. 51), however, we note that Palladio preferred to attach superimposed pairs of columns instead of single columns to the piers, and this arrangement included superimposed niches.[70]

The proportions of the nave elevation of the Redentore are approximately the same as those of the Church of Sant'Andrea in Mantua[71] and the Gesù in Rome. Palladio, however, did not follow Raphael's plan faithfully, much less the Roman thermae constructions; he clearly intended to broaden the wall surfaces within which he could easily sink the niches which he had "invented" in reconstructing the ancient "cella"[72] and which he had earlier introduced into San Giorgio Maggiore, framing the lateral walls of the principal nave and the transept.[73] The origin of the motif of stretches of wall with superimposed niches and its transformation may go back to Bramante's crossing piers, which unquestionably exercised a considerable influence on Palladio; the beveled piers of the Redentore immediately recall those of

St. Peter's. Also, Bramante's minor churches — such as San Celso and San Biagio della Pagnotta — recall this motif.[74] Renaissance church architecture, permeated with Bramantesque classicism, seems on the whole to have played a decisive part in Palladio's conception of the space under the Redentore's dome. Leaving aside the oblique shapes of the piers and considering instead the structure of the whole presbytery, a comparison with the monumental choir of Santa Maria delle Grazie, destined as a mausoleum for Lodovico Sforza, is particularly interesting; there, as in the triconch of the Redentore, the lateral apses are closely related to each other while the apse of the choir is isolated as in Palladio's church, although in a different way. A differentiation between the lateral apses and the main apse also appears in the centrally-planned construction of Santa Maria della Consolazione near Todi, which is likewise a votive church.

The articulation of the interior of the Redentore's drum also shows a direct dependence on the architecture of Bramante: Palladio's solution was certainly formulated almost literally on the exterior articulation of the drum of the Tempietto at San Pietro in Montorio. Behind the balustrade, which is formed of small bipartite balusters, the wall of the drum is articulated by pilasters into sixteen sections. Rectangular windows are opened vertically into the principal intercolumniations, while each of the other surfaces is decorated with a niche.[75] If the exterior articulation of Bramante's drum were transferred to the interior, the only difference would lie in the arrangement of the windows, which Palladio — following Venetian tradition — opens along the diagonal axes. The particular importance of Bramante's architecture for Palladio's development is also confirmed by the fact that Palladio includes the Tempietto in the fourth book of the *Quattro Libri*, which is devoted to ancient temples, as the only modern sacred building (Fig. XVI, p. 52).[76]

Nevertheless, the influence of Venetian tradition cannot be denied in Palladio's unarticulated internal dome. The origin of the form can be traced to the byzantinizing domes that were rediscovered in Venetian architecture during the Renaissance.[77] Regardless of the architectonic articulation of the drum, Palladio's dome maintains the typically Venetian effect of a weightless covering. The oculus below the lantern can be linked both to the ancient type of building like the Pantheon which is open to the sky, and to Roman church architecture of the early Cinquecento, such as Sant'Eligio degli Orefici.

Palladio had already used pilasters of the giant order to articulate the apsidal walls in the Church of San Giorgio, as well as windows superimposed on two storeys, even if only in the lateral intercolumniations. A study of general relationships has demonstrated that local tradition, Benedictine buildings of northern Italy, and influences from the works of Michelangelo converged to prepare Palladio's solution for the apses of San Giorgio.[78] However, as noted above, since the lateral apses of the Redentore do not serve to contain altars, the two-storey windows continue around them uninterruptedly in such a way that the apsidal walls recall to some extent a secular type of façade.

In Palladio's treatise the motif of niches with pediments alternating in a continuous succession and united by the common elements of bases and entablatures usually appears on walls which assume a double external-internal function: i.e., they appear as facing a space without actually serving as the element which encloses it.[79] Palladio's evident intention was to confer this particular character on the apsidal walls. In fact, the latter seem to take on the same function as the backs of either the doge's

throne or the senators' stalls in the Senate or the Grand Council rooms of the Doge's Palace. The generic derivation of this architectural motif thus does not derive from the articulation of a palace façade, such as that of the Palazzo Valmarana, transferred to a semicircular plan.

In his treatise Palladio does not articulate the monumental "backdrop" of the Roman basilica — i.e., the apse which surrounds the "luogo del Tribunale" — or, if he does do so, it is only through the "ornamenti" which he had previously mentioned. In the Belvedere Court Bramante had earlier planned and begun a "backdrop" of a type that could be called Palladian, although it was developed on a single storey and referred back to secular performances. During Palladio's first stay in Rome (1541) Bramante's design with its large niche had already been executed by Peruzzi, and in later years Michelangelo embellished the original façade with windows and added an upper storey.[80] Palladio's drawings reconstructing the Temple of Fortuna Primigenia at Palestrina[81] and his studies for the reconstruction of the Temple of Hercules Victor[82] demonstrate that the motif of the isolated "nicchio grande" was already known to him, and — knowing his admiration for Bramante — we may assume that he had carefully studied the Belvedere Court. The idea of transforming Bramante's motif in accordance with his own ideas might have been suggested to Palladio by Michelangelo; such an influence is recognizable in the construction of the walls in the lateral apses, and in the details of the elements which articulate them.

However, the design of the main apse is completely in contrast to Michelangelesque concepts. It has been repeatedly noted how, both in Cinquecento architecture and in Palladio's own work, the motif of the colonnade between two spaces derives from Roman thermae.[83] In Palladio's drawings of

Roman baths, the rectilinear shape of the colonnades is always replaced by a curvilinear — almost a semicircular — arrangement wherever the spaces open into bordering courts, i.e., wherever the spatial sequences terminate in some manner.[84] If we restricted ourselves to these examples, we would have to admit that Palladio chose the entrance or egress area of a thermal complex for the main altar of the church. Furthermore, we must not forget that, unlike a segmented thermal plan, the main apse of the Redentore forms an exact semicircle which inherently suggests its own completion by a series of columns closing the circle. If we accept the idea that Palladio did not arrive by accident at the motifs which he borrowed from antiquity, but instead kept in mind the actual significance of the ancient structures — as the first chapters of the fourth book of his *Quattro Libri* demonstrate — then we must interpret the colonnade of the Redentore as one half of a circular temple. Palladio often mentions the preëminent significance of the circular temple, with or without a cella, referring explicitly to the religious connotations of this structural form.[85] If we consider a circular monopteral temple as the generic prototype of the Redentore's colonnade, then the main altar is no longer situated "in front of an exit" but is placed at the center of a temple, nobly isolated rather like a sanctum sanctorum, lending the structure its profoundest significance, and marking the goal of the votive procession.

In the fifth chapter of the fourth book of his treatise, Palladio mentions the monopteral temple, setting forth Vitruvius's ideas: the height of the columns which rise from the base must correspond to the external diameter of the peristyle, the diameter of the columns must measure a tenth of their height, and so on. Palladio then proceeds to set forth his own observations. For the construction of a mo-

nopteron it is more advantageous — he says — to employ columns without a socle as this achieves, among other things, "maggior grandezza e magnificenza." The placing of an altar at the center of this type of circular temple,[86] the perimeter of which is a series of columns supporting the dome, enriches the motif of the special type of monopteron inasmuch as the structure can be understood as a sort of domical canopy over the altar. This fact, as well as Palladio's abovementioned observation that columns without a socle increase the "grandezza e magnificenza" of an edifice, confirms that the architect attributed a distinctive value to the monopteron motif.

Considered from this point of view, the borrowing of the motif for the shape of the main apse seems especially significant. Formally, a semi-monopteron is, so to speak, a structure able to function as an apse placed in the way that this one is, allowing communication with the monks' choir. Palladio, employing a form derived from the sacred architecture of antiquity, succeeded primarily in giving greater significance to the space that had to accommodate the main altar of the church.

Even the individual structural ratios of the colonnaded apse, which define the organism, recall the monopteron. The height of the columns (11.5 meters) corresponds to the external diameter of the apsidal semicircle, i.e., to the "diametro del minor giro de li gradi" of a monopteron; the diameter of the columns here also measures "la decima parte della loro altezza."[87] Perhaps this would also explain the slight additional height of the giant order in the Redentore relative to the ratio of the Corinthian order called for by Palladio in the treatise.[88] If the exedra is hypothetically completed to form a circle, the main altar would be enclosed exactly in its center, i.e., in the center of an imaginary monopteron (we should, of course, refer to

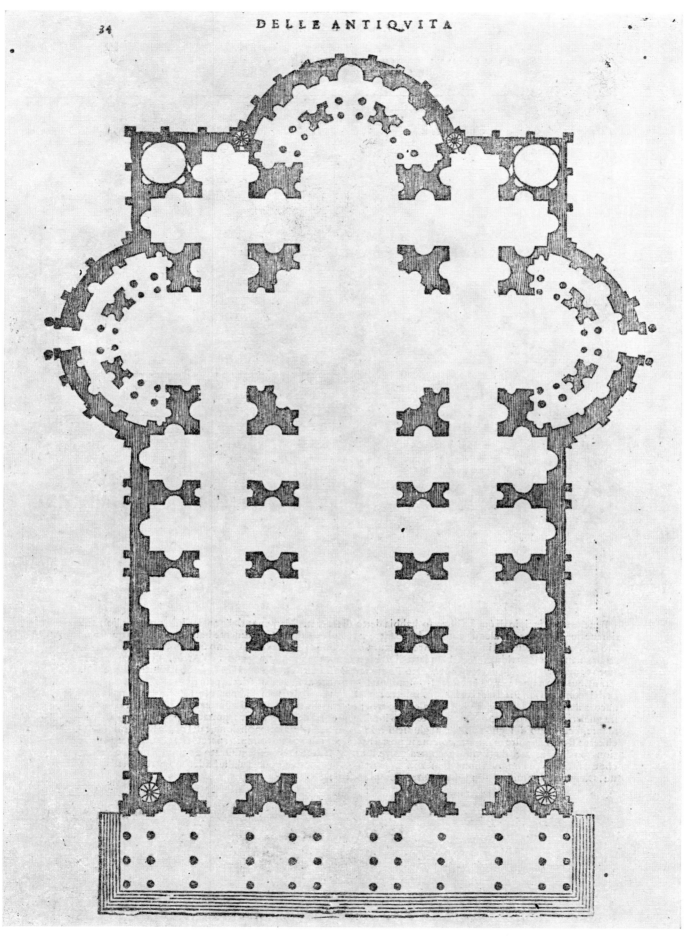

XIII - SEBASTIANO SERLIO, *Plan of St. Peter's, after Raphael.*
From *Il Terzo Libro di Sebastiano Serlio Bolognese,* Venice, 1562

the original altar and not to the present one, which dates from the Baroque period).

Wittkower interprets Palladio's church façades as the result of superimposing antique temple fronts: a low, wide front is intersected by another wider and more monumental one.[89] Pane is opposed to this theory,[90] emphasizing that a joining of two complete temple façades would represent a mechanical process. According to Pane's thesis, Palladio did not plan his façades according to that scheme, but started with the idea of a façade articulated on three surfaces and then tried to find the exact proportional ratios between the central part and the lateral walls connected to it. To support his thesis, Pane shows the absurd proportional ratios between the socle, the columns, and the pediment of what could be called the minor, or lower, façade of San Francesco della Vigna, reproduced by Wittkower in a schematic drawing as an example of two interpenetrating temple fronts. It must be emphasized above all that an interpretation here of the genesis of the façade as the superimposition of two precise and already-defined architectonic schemes stresses the façade's role as a structure independent of the rest of the church. But the organic quality of the Redentore's entire structure derives from a strict unity between interior and exterior, and this unity is in direct contrast to the interpretation that Wittkower gives of the genesis of the Palladian façade.[91]

We have attempted elsewhere to examine the configuration of a Palladian basilical church façade.[92] Palladio's ideas seem to have been strongly influenced on the one hand by medieval church façades in the Veneto, with their accentuated vertical tripartition, and by Venetian Renaissance churches in which the façade anticipates the internal spatial structure; on the other hand, he also profited from study of both façades with porticoes[93] and those of an-

tique temples. Insofar as this particular formal representation is concerned, another reflection which plainly appears in a sentence by Palladio in his chapter "Del Compartimento de i Tempii" is important: "Ma noi, lasciati i portici intorno, edifichiamo li Tempij, che si assimigliano molto alle Basiliche, nelle quali, come è stato detto, si facevano i portici nella parte di dentro, come noi facciamo hora ne i Tempij."[94] The four giant columns with a pediment, a characteristic motif of Palladian façades, demonstrate externally the indisputable relationship between temple and basilica and — more precisely — the affinity of the Christian basilica to the temple, which Palladio had set forth theoretically in the passage quoted above. This "temple front" anticipates the interior space, and its structure is conditioned by the latter in a manner so logical and so artistically perfect that the problem of the "applied portico" becomes unimportant.

If we compare the façade of the Redentore with that of San Giorgio Maggiore, which was designed earlier, we can see a difference which is not merely stylistic. The traditional North Italian vertical tripartition, accentuated by the projection of the central element, is evident. The "square columns" on one hand and the distribution of the various elements on planes varying in depth and height on the other contribute to the clear formulation of the fundamental compositional concept. The stimulus for this mode of composition — which, as was noted in the description of the exterior of the church, determines a vertical progression in the façade's articulation appropriately terminating in the dome — was no doubt derived from Palladio's study of thermal architecture. Among the architect's drawings are not only plans and sections of thermae, as we have discussed above, but also a series of sheets (Fig. XII, p. 41) with the aid of

XIV - ANDREA PALLADIO, *design for a façade.* London, R.I.B.A., XIV/10

which he evidently sought to study and clarify the external aspect of these structures with their multiple articulations (such as intersecting pediments, exterior walls rising from different levels, and so on).[95] Confronted by these very sober reconstructions of the exteriors of Roman thermal complexes, we can understand even better the construction of the Redentore's façade, which obeys the principle of the articulation in depth of the various elements.

A new motif appears in the church's façade, i.e., the attic; it is absent from the façade of San Giorgio Maggiore and as a motif derives from the front of the Pantheon.[96] As the attic in this case is part of the wall corresponding to the nave of the church and not to the space beneath the dome, as is the case in the Pantheon, Palladio's use of it must signify a surmounting of the motif itself, freed from its original associations.

It cannot be excluded that Palladio, in planning the Redentore, also kept in mind certain solutions seen in the Pantheon. However, the necessity of placing a basilical nave before a centralized body constituted a problem quite remote from the porticoed façade of the Pantheon, which to the architect's eyes did not represent the ancient building's original state in any case. Sections of the Baths of Agrippa show, among other things, a basilical space behind which the dome of the Pantheon rises.[97] If we compare this with the Redentore, the latter's façade had to be planned for its basilical space and not for its area with a circular plan. If, on the basis of the considerations set forth above, it does not seem possible to maintain that the columns of the Redentore façade were meant to reproduce the portico of the Pantheon, we also cannot undertake to derive the attic from the section of wall which appears in the Pantheon as an attic above the portico, considerably recessed from the front.

Considering the relationship between the attic and the lower part of the Redentore's façade and observing that behind the pediment the attic rises perceptibly above the entablature of the order, one might recall a generic relationship which has not yet been considered. If we think of the interior space of the Redentore — i.e., the nave behind the façade — as a "via triumphalis" accompanied by gigantic structural ornamentation, and if we consider its function as being that of receiving a pro-cession, it will then be clear that a borrow-ing on Palladio's part of the triumphal arch motif would be not only explicable but justified. The diversity of the intercolum-niations in the central part of the present façade does not correspond according to the principle of "rhythmic *travée*" to the precepts expressed by Palladio himself in his treatise, nor is it met in his examples of antique temples. Palladio does not take a stand on whether or not an association between the façade of a "Christian temple" and a triumphal arch is permissible, and we wish here only to suggest the possi-bility of such a generic derivation. In any case, a drawing by the architect does exist (Fig. XIV, p. 47) in which the motif of a triumphal arch is flanked by two lower units in just the same arrangement that is found in Palladian church façades.[98]

b) The Chiesa del Redentore, right flank

NOTES

[1] The method employed in this study was suggested by the conviction that every true work of art " is something original and individual, not simply an examble of a type." Cf. SEDLMAYR, 1958, pp. 95 ff.

[2] Cf. also the recent book by ZORZI, 1967, pp. 121 ff.

[3] Archivio di Stato, Venice - *Senato Terra*, F. 70.

[4] Archivio di Stato, Venice - *Senato Terra*, R. 51 and *Cerimoniali* I. Cf. Appendix III, n. 1.

[5] Archivio di Stato, Venice - *Cerimoniali* I. Cf. Appendix III, n. 2.

[6] Archivio di Stato, Venice - *Senato Terra*, F. 70. Agostino Barbarigo and Antonio Bragadin were chosen as *provveditori*. Cf. Appendix III, n. 3.

[7] Archivio di Stato, Venice - *Senato Terra*, R. 51. Cf. Appendix III, n. 4. A Venetian pace corresponds to 5 *piedi*; a Venetian *piede* corresponds to about 0.3477 meters.

[8] Archivio di Stato, Venice - *Senato Terra*, F. 70.

[9] The area in which the since-destroyed Church and Convent of Santa Croce were located can be clearly located on Jacopo de' Barbari's map.

[10] Archivio di Stato, Venice - *Senato Terra*, F. 70, three appendices accompanying the minutes of the sitting of November 17, 1576.

[11] King David replied to the Jebusite Ornan, who had offered him his threshing floor without payment so that he could erect the altar there, " Nay; but I will verily buy it for the full price: for I will not take that which is thine for the Lord, nor offer burnt offerings without cost " (I Chronicles 21: 24).

[12] Archivio di Stato, Venice - *Cerimoniali* I. Cf. Appendix III, n. 7.

[13] Archivio di Stato, Venice - *Senato Terra*, F. 70, first appendix to the minutes of November 17, 1576: " che essendo venuto del ordine delli clarissimi Bragadin et Barbarigo l'architetto Ruschoni al nostro monasterio per far una pianta per lo edificar detta chiesa; Fò principiato esso dessegno al pozzo, che è sopra il nostro Campo, et entrando con una picciol parte nel detto monasterio et Chiesa nostra riusciva un Tempio molto più bello, et amplo, che quello di Santa Maria Maggiore, si come per essa pianta veder si può. "

[14] Archivio di Stato, Venice - *Senato Terra*, F. 70.

[15] TEMANZA, 1762, p. lxiii, states that the *provveditori* also took into consideration the site on which the now-deconsecrated Church of Santa Maria Maggiore is located.

[16] Archivio di Stato, Venice - *Senato Terra*, F. 70, appendix to the minutes of November 17, 1576.

[17] Archivio di Stato, Venice - *Senato Terra*, F. 70.

[18] According to ZORZI, 1967, p. 124: " We certainly cannot maintain that the representations of temples shown in the three *oselle* coined in 1576 are preliminary projects. " In regard to the question of the *oselle* in relation to the Redentore, see Appendix II.

[19] Archivio di Stato, Venice - *Senato Terra*, F. 70. Cf. Appendix III, n. 5.

[20] Archivio di Stato, Venice - *Notatorio Collegio* I, F. 60. Cf. Appendix III, n. 6.

[21] One of the functions of the " Magistrato al Sal " was that of financing work on public buildings for the Republic.

[22] Cf. also the contrary opinion of SINDING-LARSEN, 1965, pp. 419-437.

[23] Archivio di Stato, Venice - *Notatorio Collegio* I, F. 60. Cf. Appendix III, n. 6.

[24] The most apt example is offered by San Giorgio Maggiore in Venice, the model of which was completed only a few days before the laying of the first stone. Cf. MAGRINI, 1845, pp. 62 ff.

[25] Cf. BETTO, 1943, p. 88. In the opinion of Rodolfo Pallucchini, the author of the painting is Alessandro Varotari, called " il Padovanino " (oral communication).

[26] The very obvious resemblance to the portrait of Doge Alvise Mocenigo painted by Tintoretto (now in the Accademia in Venice) leaves no doubt concerning the identification.

[27] Archivio di Stato, Venice - *Senato Terra*, F. 70.

[28] Archivio di Stato, Venice - *Senato Terra*, F. 83, appendix to the decree of November 11, 1581.

[29] Cf. DA PORTOGRUARO, 1930, pp. 160 ff.

[30] Cf. Appendix III, n. 1.

[31] According to an entry of August 6, 1577, the owners of the land — " nobili nostri Lippomano " — were paid 3,750 ducats in all. Archivio di Stato, Venice - *Notatorio Collegio*, R. 42.

[32] In addition to the doge, the patriarch of Aquileja, Giovanni Grimani, gave 1,000 ducats for the votive church and the future *provveditore* Antonio Bragadin 500 ducats on September 4, 1576. Archivio di Stato, Venice - *Senato Terra*, R. 51.

[33] Archivio di Stato, Venice - *Senato Terra*, R. 52.

[34] Archivio di Stato, Venice - *Senato Terra*, F. 79.

[35] This statement confirms that in the sitting of the Senate of February 9, 1577, they did not hold merely a general discussion about the form of the church, but chose between well-defined projects.

[36] Archivio di Stato, Venice - *Senato Terra*, R. 51. Cf. Appendix III, n. 8.

[37] Archivio di Stato, Venice - *Cerimoniali*, I. Cf. Appendix III, n. 9.

[38] Cf. STRINGA, 1604, p. 188 v.

[39] The letter is published in the appendix to the first volume of the *Raccolta di Lettere*, ed. BOTTARI, 1822, n. XLV, without any citation of source. The date is given only as 1577. The authenticity of the letter has often been questioned.

[40] The colored stucco decoration of these rectangles — the Cross of the Consecration — must be considered an extraneous addition to the original concept.

[41] STRINGA, 1604, p. 188 v., reports that the placing of statues in the niches between the half-columns had been envisaged. While Palladio was still alive, the first statues were placed in the niches of the front interior wall of San Giorgio Maggiore. Cf. CESSI, 1961, p. 47. In a drawing of the elevation of a church interior (R.I.B.A., XIV, 14) in which narrow sections of wall similar to those in the Redentore appear, Palladio also places statues in the niches. Cf. TIMOFIEWITSCH, 1959-60, pp. 79-87,

fig. 107. Between 1619 and 1620 grisailles (painted by Paolo Piazza) of Sibyls, Prophets, Evangelists, and Fathers of the Church were placed in the Redentore's niches.

[42] Cf. BERTOTTI-SCAMOZZI, 1796, Vol. IV, p. 11.

[43] PALLADIO, 1570, Bk. I, Ch. 23.

[44] Cf. ZARLINO, 1562, pp. 23, 158 ff.; WITTKOWER, 1962, pp. 111 ff.

[45] In the opinion Palladio gave on the model of the Duomo of Brescia, he speaks of a " colonna quadra," which indicates that the term would have been generally understood. Palladio's opinion is published by MAGRINI, 1845, Appendix, pp. 12-16.

[46] In 1604 STRINGA, p. 192, reported that the church was " fabricata su il modello del Palladio ma fu fornita dal bozzetto."

[47] The Capuchins' protests were silenced only by a special brief of Gregory XIII. Cf. Archivio di Stato, Venice - *Dispacci Roma*, F. 12, p. 591.

[48] The interior of the church must, of course, have been conceived without the mystical darkness produced by the red curtains, which prevent light from entering.

[49] Cf. n. 45.

[50] The stair, as well as the platform, is surrounded by a balustrade, the balusters of which become wider at the bottom like a vase; this reveals, however, that it was not constructed at the same time the church was built, but that it is a later addition of the second half of the seventeenth century. The appearance of balustrades of this type in Venetian architecture is connected with the activity of Longhena and one of the first examples is the balustrade around the exterior of the drum at Santa Maria della Salute. Since in the years 1673-74 the statues for the façade of the Redentore were also entrusted to the group of sculptors who worked on the Church of Santa Maria della Salute (cf. Appendix I), it might be conjectured — keeping in mind the abovementioned formal analogies — that the Redentore's stair parapet was built at approximately the same time. The votive painting of the doge Alvise Mocenigo with the reproduction of the model of the Redentore (Fig. XVII, p. 57), as well as the view of the church (Fig. XXIII, p. 64) in an engraving of 1610 by Franco (folio 9), both show the flight of stairs in front of the façade without a parapet.

[51] The premise that there is a common concept at the basis of the whole work naturally applies.

[52] HOFFMANN, 1938, p. 94.

[53] Cf. PANE, 1961, p. 299 and HUBALA, 1965, pp. 926-930.

[54] Archivio di Stato, Venice - *Cerimoniali* I, folio lx.

[55] *La liberazione di Vinegia* (*Di Vinegia alli 22 luglio 1577*). The Biblioteca Marciana has two copies of this eyewitness report written in the form of a letter. Cf. Appendix III, no. 10.

[56] The place where the since-destroyed Church of San Giovanni della Giudecca was located can be found on the de' Barbari map. Cf. Appendix III, no. 9.

[57] Archivio di Stato, Venice - *Cerimoniali* I, folio lxxv. Cf. Appendix III, no. 11.

[58] In the Museo Civico Correr, Venice.

[59] Cf. the contrary opinion of IVANOFF, 1967, p. 89: " Whoever views the church from the opposite bank of the Zattere sees it frontally on just one plane, without any impression of surface movement. "

[60] SANSOVINO-STRINGA, 1604, p. 340.

[61] PALLADIO, 1570, Bk. I, Ch. 18.

[62] The purpose of these spaces is also pointed out by STRINGA, 1604, p. 188 v.; " Nelle braccia della crociera vi sono alcuni sedili di legname di noce fatti fare per il Doge e per la Signoria, quando se ne viene ogni anno la terza Domenica di Luglio a visitar questo Tempio. "

[63] The theory of SINDING-LARSEN, 1965, p. 430, according to which the building of the Redentore " points clearly to a hasty adaption of the original project rather than the substitution of a completely new one, " could derive only from an evaluation of Palladio as a classicist. On the other hand, the idea that the nave of the Redentore had been added to the plan of the central body in the space of just one week is contradictory to architectural practice. Naturally Sinding-Larsen is right when he maintains that, notwithstanding the requirements necessitated by the " vow," the " forma rotonda " was still under discussion in 1577. But it is not at all certain that the project provided the shape and dimensions of the present space under the dome. This project would not in any way have satisfied the conditions required of a votive, processional, and conventual church.

[64] In the abovementioned opinion of the " maggior Schola di theologi et canonisti, che oggidi si trova in questa Città " explicit reference was made, along with the citation of a long series of theological considerations, to the " mistero della Croce in questo flagello della peste. "

[65] Cf. also ACKERMAN, 1966, pp. 132 ff. FORSSMAN'S assertion, 1965, p. 118, that the basilica at Fano might have influenced the planimetric concept of the Redentore is not convincing if one considers the importance of the longitudinal axis in the Redentore's plan and the church's spatial conception.

[66] Cf. ZORZI, 1958, figs. 84-145 and SPIELMANN, 1966.

[67] Cf. HEYDENREICH, 1938, p. 273.

[68] Cf. WITTKOWER, 1962, p. 99.

[69] Cf. ZORZI, 1958, fig. 132 and p. 71; SPIELMANN, 1966, p. 72.

[70] Cf. ZORZI, 1958, fig. 128.

[71] Cf. HUBALA, 1961, p. 103, n. 28.

[72] In his description of temples in the *Quattro Libri*, Palladio recognizes that those which have been preserved do not furnish any evidence regarding the articulation of the internal walls of the cella. Concerning his illustrations of them in the treatise, he remarks: " Io ve ne ho fatto di mia inventione." Cf. PALLADIO, 1570, Bk. IV, Chs. 7 and 10.

[73] Cf. TIMOFIEWITSCH, 1967, pp. 13 ff.

[74] Cf. FÖRSTER, 1956, figs. 83, 88.

[75] In Palladio's San Giorgio Maggiore, begun eleven years before the Redentore, rectangular and arched niches alternate in the wall of the drum exactly as at Bramante's Tempietto.

[76] PALLADIO, 1570, Bk. IV, Ch. 17.

[77] Cf. TIMOFIEWITSCH, 1964, pp. 271-282.

[78] Cf. TIMOFIEWITSCH, 1967, pp. 45 ff.

[79] Palladio makes use of this motif (Bk. IV, Ch. 12) in his reconstruction of the Temple of Jupiter (cf. PANE, 1948, p. 104), especially in the interior part of the wall that surrounds the court of the temple. A variant of this motif appears also in his reconstruction of the so-called Temple of Minerva Medica (Bk. IV, Ch. 11), and, what is even more interesting, the motif in this case is applied to the interior walls of spaces annexed to a round temple in an apse-like fashion, separated from the central area by colonnades.

[80] ACKERMAN, 1954, pp. 61, 75 ff.

[81] Cf. ZORZI, 1958, figs. 200, 201.

[82] Cf. ZORZI, 1958, figs. 205, 206, 209, 210.

[83] Cf. SIEBENHÜNER, 1955, pp. 179-206 and SPIELMANN, 1966, p. 70.

[84] Cf. ZORZI, 1958, figs. 84, 96, 106.

[85] PALLADIO, 1570, Bk. IV, Chs. 2 and 5.

[86] PALLADIO, 1570, Bk. IV, Ch. 5, " ... nel mezo de' quali si poneva l'altare."

[87] PALLADIO, 1570, Bk. IV, Ch. 5.

[88] PALLADIO, 1570, Bk. I, Ch. 17.

[89] WITTKOWER, 1962, pp. 89 ff.

[90] PANE, 1956, pp. 408-412.

[91] Cf. PANE, 1961, p. 299.

[92] Cf. TIMOFIEWITSCH, 1967, pp. 49 ff.

[93] As is demonstrated by his reconstruction of the Basilica of Maxentius.

[94] PALLADIO, 1570, Bk. IV, Ch. 5.

[95] Cf. ZORZI, 1958, figs. 85, 86, 93, 94, 98, 129.

[96] WITTKOWER, 1962, p. 93.

[97] Cf. ZORZI, 1958, fig. 143.

[98] Cf. FORSSMAN, 1965, fig. 51 and pp. 113-114.

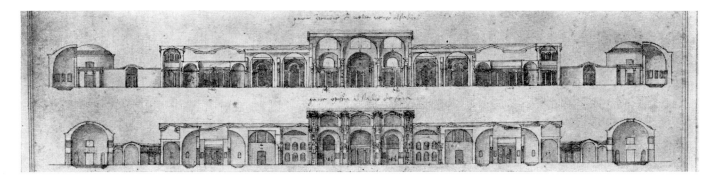

XV - ANDREA PALLADIO, *Baths of Diocletian, detail of a section.* London, R.I.B.A., V/2

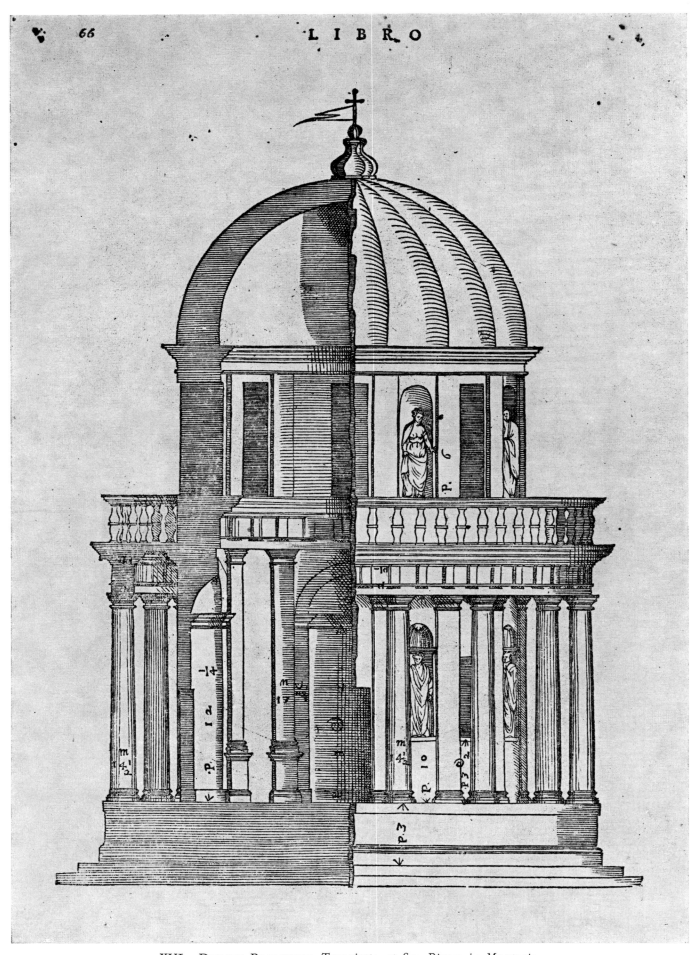

XVI - Donato Bramante, *Tempietto at San Pietro in Montorio.*
From I *Quattro Libri dell'Architettura di Andrea Palladio*, Bk. IV, Ch. 17, Venice, 1570

This first appendix offers a brief account of the decoration of the interior and façade of the church. The only works considered are those which are contemporary with the church's construction and thus form part of the original concept, or those later ones which can nevertheless be linked with the fundamental idea that conditions the whole complex.[1]

Seven statues of Istrian stone decorate the façade: two are in the niches flanking the entrance portal, representing St. Mark on the left (Plate 12) and St. Francis of Assisi on the right (Plate 13). Above the cornice of the central section are three other statues: in the center an allegory of Faith, and at the corners kneeling angels. Two additional statues are set on the outer corners of the lateral sections; on the left is San Lorenzo Giustiniani and on the right St. Anthony of Padua (Plate 11). Thus the patron saints of the city to which the church belonged and of the Order entrusted with the care of the church balance each other.

These statues were executed long after the construction of the façade. In his description of the Redentore, Stringa confirms that at the beginning of the Seicento there was still no sculpture on the church's façade.[2] This is confirmed by the oldest known view of the church (Fig. XXIII, p. 64), in an engraving by G. Franco.[3] It shows only a statue of Christ as Redeemer on the lantern of the dome, which was also cited by Stringa; the latter reports that sculptural decoration was planned for the façade, but not even the Martinioni edition of his work mentions it.[4]

G. Lorenzetti attributed the statues of St. Mark and St. Francis in the lower section to the Veronese sculptor Girolamo Campagna.[5] Stylistic characteristics aside, however, numerous documents testify that the sculptural decoration of the façade was only begun in 1673,[6] a good forty-five years after Campagna's death.

In a request to the Senate on April 28, 1673, the *Provveditori al Sal*,[7] following the wishes of the Capuchins themselves, proposed that " cinque statue di marmo " be placed on the façade of the Redentore. The proposal was accepted on May 5th of the same year, and at the same time it was arranged that the execution of the sculptures was to be handled in agreement with the " deputati sopra la fabrica della Chiesa della Salute." [8]

Although the façade today has seven statues, only five are cited in the abovementioned documents. The text of the decree indicated where the five figures were to be placed: " tre per riportar nella sommità della stessa facciata, e due ne li nicchi alle pareti. " It is therefore demonstrable that in 1673 the sculptural decoration of only the central section of the façade was under consideration. If we compare the individual statues, the saints in the niches and the kneeling angels at the upper corners of the central section show a strong formal resemblance to each other. Furthermore, the stylistic connections of these statues with the sculpture on the exterior of Santa Maria della Salute are quite evident, proving that the Senate's order was actually followed. The question remains open of whether or not this stylistic agreement with the Santa Maria della Salute decoration justifies the attribution of the Redentore's statues to the workshop of the Flemish sculptor Josse de Corte (also called Giusto Le Curt), active in Venice between 1650 and 1675.[9] The two statues of San Lorenzo Giustiniani and St. Anthony of Padua are not mentioned in the decree of May 5, 1673, and differ stylistically from the abovementioned group. Their less agitated outline and the softly vibrant treatment of surfaces suggests that they belong to a later period, i.e., around 1700. Views of the church made after 1700 — such as that by Luca Carlevaris in his *Le fabriche*,[10] or Canaletto's painting in the Duke of Bedford's collection,[11] or the engraving in the *Forestiere illuminato*[12] — show the façade of the Redentore as already containing seven statues.

The lead panels of the door were executed after a design by Zandomenico Gornizai in 1667.[13]

On entering the church, we note at either side of the entrance two holy-water fonts, with high bases shaped like vases and wide, low basins; they are part of the original furnishings of the church and are mentioned in Stringa's description.[14] At the beginning of the Seicento a small bronze statue was placed in the center of each basin; in the one at the right of the entrance is the figure of the Redeemer (Plate 6), and in that at the left is the figure of St. John the Baptist (Plate 62).[15]

The altarpieces follow a strict Christological program, which begins in the first chapel on the right with a *Nativity* by Francesco Bassano (Plate 64).[16] The *Baptism of Christ* (school of Veronese; Plate 65) follows in the second chapel,[17] and the *Flagellation* (school of Tintoretto; Plate 66)[18] is in the last chapel on the same side. Above the main altar is a statue of the crucified Christ (Plate 56). The *Entombment* by Palma il Giovane (Plate 67)[19] follows in the first chapel on the left of the nave counting from the crossing, and the *Resurrection* by Francesco Bassano (Plates 68, 70)[20] is in the next chapel. The cycle is completed by the *Ascension* (workshop of Tintoretto; Plate 69).[21]

This iconological arrangement reflects the movement of the procession on the day of the *Festa del Redentore*: accompanied by the episodes from the life of Christ, it progressed toward the main altar where " nel passar della processione le genti facessero riverentia et oratione per ditta liberatione ";[22] then it proceeded back down toward the exit.

The simple aedicular form of the side altars (Plate 28) certainly goes back to a Palladian idea.[23] A comparison with an autograph drawing by the master in London showing a church interior confirms this.[24] The form of the side altar on this sheet substantially agrees with that of the altars in the Redentore.

The main altar (Plate 55), however, no longer exists in its original form. The present structure rises above five steps in three planes; it consists of an elongated altar slab and a central section decorated with small spiral columns, on which the cross with the bronze figure of Christ is erected. Its execution dates to 1680-81.[25]

We may obtain an idea of the original altar's appearance from Stringa's description. Above the marble slab to which five steps led, as we still see today, rose a large tabernacle supported on the shoulders (" con gli homeri sostenuto ") of four angels placed at the corners. This, according to Stringa, was " di vaghissimi intagli ornato, con colonne, angioletti, festoni, fogliami, cornici, " etc. It was also decorated with small paintings, " due per ogni facciata."[26] From the petition for the erection of a new main altar, formulated by the Capuchins and addressed to the Signoria on August 23, 1679,[27] we learn that the upper part of the original altar had been made " di legno indorato." Above the tabernacle rose the present " grande, e grossa Croce di forte e duro legno, tutta indorata con un Christo crocifisso di bronzo " (Plate 56). On either side of the altar slab were two other bronze figures — St. Mark on the left (Plate 59), and St. Francis on the right (Plate 60) — which, like the Crucifix, were reinserted into the new main altar.[28]

Stringa informs us that on the back of the cross the inscription *Franciscus Mazol. Fusor* could be read; he conjectures that this artist was the author of all three bronze statues. However, as the inscription clearly indicates, the signature is not that of the sculptor but of the master who did the casting; and in a letter of June 19, 1604, to the Duke of Urbino, Girolamo Campagna lists the sculptures of the main altar of the Redentore among his works.[29]

Also reinserted into the new main altar were marble sections of the old altar, such as the low, stepped platform and the altar slab. On the sides at the bottom one can clearly distinguish the outline of the bases and cornice of the older mid-section, which was cut in a much more delicate manner than the richly articulated and decisively cut edges of the marble slabs added later.

Besides incorporating the three large bronze figures by Girolamo Campagna that were part of the original altar (the crucified Christ with the two patron saints of the city and the Capuchin Order at his feet as intercessors), the Baroque design embellished the altar with additional sculptural decoration. The two upper levels contain a whole series of small bronze statues:[30] the two Princes of the Apostles appear in the front of the central section and higher up, on the small balustrade of the central section, are the Doctors of the Church and the two protectors against the plague, St. Roch and St. Sebastian (Plate 57). Just beneath the Crucifix are half-reclining figures of angels holding the Instruments of the Passion, and in the lower part of the altar (i.e., in the altar block) are two marble reliefs. On the front is a scene of Christ carrying the Cross (Plate 58), and on the back, facing the monks' choir, is that of the Deposition.[31]

The new sculptures are in complete accord with the original iconographic scheme of the interior. The two reliefs showing Christ carrying the Cross and the Deposition are thematically inserted between the Flagellation in the last chapel on the right, the Crucifixion on the main altar, and the Entombment in the chapel on the left; this broadens the original iconographic scheme and at the same time exalts the central point of the program, Christ's death on the Cross. The statues of the two Princes of the Apostles (the founders of the Christian Church), of the Doctors of the Church (witnesses to its tradition), and of the angels with the symbols of the Passion — disposed one above the other following the architectural construction of the altar — emphasize once again the specialized thematic arrangement of the decoration of the high altar within the context of the general program. With the insertion of the two saints who protect against the plague (Sts. Roch and Sebastian), the motif of intercession — which can be considered the secondary iconological theme of the high altar — is developed on a vertical axis and achieves its full force. Reading the Christological theme (which runs along the longitudinal axis and belongs to both major spaces) together with the theme of intercession on the high altar, one is fully able to recognize the fundamental concept which determined the entire interior iconological program: the redemption obtained through the death of Christ on the Cross. This same idea had given birth to the Senate's vow and from that came its elaboration in the Palladian building.

In addition to the paintings previously cited, there are two others on the entrance wall of the church (Plate 23). One is inserted into the blind semicircular arch over the portal, the other is in the lunette of the barrel vault. The two paintings date from the Seicento and are not directly linked to the original iconological program. The upper painting, a grisaille, shows the doge and his retinue kneeling before Christ; among the saints depicted are St. Mark and St. Francis. The painter was Padre Cosimo da Castelfranco (also known as Paolo Piazza), and the work must have been painted at approximately the same period in which Piazza executed the grisailles for the niches, i.e., in 1619-20 [32] (as has already been noted, grisaille figures of Prophets, Sibyls, Evangelists, and Fathers of the Church painted in imitation of sculpture adorned the niches until the recent restoration of the interior).[33]

The lower panel, also lunette-shaped, in the entrance wall is still later in date. It shows the Madonna with the Christ Child and St. Felix and is the work of Pietro Muttoni (called " della Vecchia "). This painting is not mentioned by Martinioni and therefore must have been executed between 1663 and Muttoni's death in 1678.

Finally, one can read on the walls of the nave a few inscriptions referring to events in the church's construction. Below the entablature on the entrance wall a wide gilded band, punctuated at each end by the Lion of St. Mark in an heraldic field, carries an inscription in elegant capitals: " CHRISTO REDEMPTORI, CIVITATE GRAVI PESTILENTIA LIBERATA, SENATUS EX VOTO. PRID. NON. SEPT. AN. MDLXXVI. " The other inscriptions are in the two first lateral intercolumniations. On the first tablet, in the right lateral wall, we read: " DVCE ALOYSIO MOCOENIGO, V. NO. MAII AN. MDLXXVII," and on the tablet opposite: " PRIMARIVS LAPIS A. IOAN TREVISANO PATRIARCA VENETIAR." The second tablet in the last intercolumniation of the right wall carries the inscription: " DVCE PASCALE CYCONIA V. KAL. OCT. AN. MDXCII," and the one on the left lateral wall reads: " CONSECRATVM A. LAVRENT. PRIOLO PATRIARCA VENETIAR." All the tablets were inserted in the nave wall before 1604, as they are mentioned by Stringa.[34]

NOTES TO APPENDIX I

[1] Concerning the works of art preserved in the sacristy of the church, see LORENZETTI, 1926, p. 723.

[2] SANSOVINO-STRINGA, 1604, p. 188.

[3] FRANCO, 1610, folio 9.

[4] SANSOVINO, 1663, p. 256.

[5] LORENZETTI, 1926, p. 722.

[6] These documents have been published by DA PORTOGRUARO, 1930, p. 173.

[7] As previously mentioned, one of the duties of the Magistrato del Sal was to supervise the Republic's public construction.

[8] Archivio di Stato, Venice - *Senato Terra*, F. 872.

[9] Cf. DA PORTOGRUARO, 1930, p. 173. In his *Zibaldone* (1738 ff.; ed. Ivanoff, 1963, p. 90), Tommaso TEMANZA cites these statues as works by the sculptor Tommaso Ruer.

[10] CARLEVARIS, 1703, pl. 3.

[11] Reproduced by MOSCHINI, 1954, fig. 99.

[12] 1740, plate following p. 268.

[13] Cf. DA PORTOGRUARO, 1930, p. 174.

[14] SANSOVINO-STRINGA, 1604, p. 188 v.

[15] Each of the two statues is signed and dated on the base: *Franciscvs Terilli Feltrinensis F. 1610*. The Senate's deliberation of July 21, 1611, mentions the payment for these statues. Archivio di Stato, Venice - *Senato Terra*, R. 81.

[16] Signed on a rock under Christ's crib: *Franc.ˢ a Ponte Bassa.ˢ Fac.*

[17] According to RIDOLFI, 1648, p. 354, the altarpiece was begun by Paolo Caliari and, after the death of the master in 1588, was finished by his collaborators and heirs, his brother Benedetto and his sons Carlo and Gabriele. The painting is signed: *Heredes Pauli Caliari vero. fecerunt.*

[18] The painting is not signed. Cf. LORENZETTI, 1926, p. 723.

[19] Signed at the lower right: *Jacobus Palma P.*

[20] Signed on a small white scroll: *Franc.ˢ Bass. F.*

[21] The painting is not signed. Cf. LORENZETTI, 1926, p. 723.

[22] Archivio di Stato, Venice - *Cerimoniali* I, fol. lx.

[23] It is perhaps interesting in this regard to recall that Goethe in his brief description of the Redentore admits Palladio's intervention in the side altars. Cf. GOETHE (annotated edition by Herbert von Einem), 1951, p. 73. The side altars were certainly finished in 1588, since on May 16th of that year the Senate granted a sum of money for their furnishing. Archivio di Stato, Venice - *Senato Terra*, R. 58.

[24] R.I.B.A., XIV/14; cf. TIMOFIEWITSCH, 1959-60, fig. 107.

[25] The baroque refurbishing of the altar goes back to a plan by the Capuchin mathematician Giuseppe da Vicenza. Cf. DA PORTOGRUARO, 1930, pp. 180 ff.

[26] These paintings from the workshop of Francesco Bassano are now in the sacristy of the church.

[27] Archivio di Stato, Venice - *Senato Terra*, F. 989.

[28] The upper part of the altar described by Stringa, supported by four cast figures, recalls the compositional arrangement of the main altar of San Giorgio Maggiore in Venice. In a senatorial decree of March 24, 1590, we read that " per il compimento della chiesa votiva del Redentor nostro alla Zudecha restando a far il pavimento, due figure di bronzo, ch'uanno sopra l'altar grande et alcuni, altre poche cose " (Archivio di Stato, Venice - *Senato Terra*, R. 60). Thus the two large bronze statues can be dated between 1590 and the consecration of the church in 1592.

[29] Cf. GRONAU, 1936, p. 244.

[30] They are the work of G. M. Mazza. Cf. RICCOMINI, 1967, pp. 173-184.

[31] Works by Tommaso Ruer. Cf. IVANOFF, 1963, p. 90.

[32] Cf. DA PORTOGRUARO, 1930, pp. 176 and 192.

[33] Cf. also GOETHE, 1786, p. 73.

[34] SANSOVINO-STRINGA, 1604, p. 188 v

XVII - *Votive painting showing the doge Alvise Mocenigo* (formerly in the Robilant collection)

XVIII - *Osella of Doge Alvise Mocenigo for 1576.* Venice, Museo Correr

XIX - *Osella of Doge Alvise Mocenigo for 1576* (unique). Venice, Museo Correr

XX - *Osella of Doge Alvise Mocenigo for 1576* (unique). Venice, Museo Correr

XXI - *Osella of Doge Alvise Mocenigo for 1576* (unique). London, British Museum

XXII - *Osella of Doge Alvise Mocenigo for 1576* (unique). London, British Museum

APPENDIX II

Oselle were special silver coins minted in Venice, distributed each year before Christmas by the doge to all the Venetian nobles who had voting rights in the Grand Council. The distribution generally took place on the feast day of St. Barbara [1] (December 4), but in some cases the doge could delay the ceremony for several days.[2] The *oselle* were not considered simply as commemorative medals but also as coins in regular circulation and were, in fact, of great value.[3] Their form was established by a decree of December 9, 1523, as follows:[4] the obverse had to contain the standing figure of St. Mark, with the kneeling figure of the doge offering him a standard, and around the edge had to be the same inscription as on the other Venetian coin in current use, the ducat; on the reverse a six-line inscription gave the name and year of the appointment of the doge donating the coin and, around the edge, the date.

This established type was faithfully followed, especially in earlier periods. The successive variants in the obverses correspond to those found in the Venetian ducat during the same years; for example, sometimes St. Mark is shown as seated. Up until 1575 the *oselle* of the doge Alvise Mocenigo were coined in accordance with the traditional scheme; then, in the following year — his seventh in office — the coins assume a completely individual form.

Various examples of the *oselle* of the year of the Senate's vow have come down to us. The differences do not stem from slight variations resulting from the minting process — as often happens in coins of this type — but rather involve five images each fundamentally different from the others. Four of these *oselle* are known in single examples,[5] but various examples survive of the fifth variant.

The fifth variant (Fig. XVIII, p. 58) has a scene analogous to the one engraved on the ducat, with the difference that the doge is no longer portrayed as kneeling before St. Mark but before the risen Christ. On the obverse the usual inscription around the edge is replaced by the six-line legend of the reverse running in a circle, while in the central area of the reverse — in place of the traditional inscription — is the representation of a two-storey building viewed from the side, with a semi-cylindrical roof. The side wall of this structure, articulated in three bays, is richly decorated with statues; above the round pediment of the façade — which recalls solutions of the Early Renaissance in Venice — is the Lion of St. Mark. The inscription that runs around the edge — " REDEMPTORI VOTUM MDLXXVI " — proclaims the Republic's vow.

Each of the four unique pieces, minted in the same year of Alvise Mocenigo's dogate, has an architectonic representation on the reverse like the *osella* previously described, although each is different from the others. The obverses in all four models again differ; only one model follows the solution of the first *osella*, which had been obtained by combining the traditional elements of the two sides. The building shown on its reverse (Fig. XX, p. 59) has a certain analogy with the actual appearance of the votive church in that it presents a façade subdivided into three sections by four vertical elements that run from the base up to the entablature; the façade, which has a flight of steps in front, is flanked by wings which are somewhat lower and very narrow. Above the triangular pediment rises the dome, set on a low drum. The inscription reads: " SALUS EX VOTO."[6] The second unique piece (Fig. XXI, p. 59) retains the ducal inscription, but not the same principal scene. The doge, with the Lion of St. Mark beside him, kneels on the bank of the Giudecca facing the risen Christ, who appears on some clouds at the right. On the other side of the canal, the Piazzetta and Doge's Palace are clearly recognizable. The reverse shows a centrally-planned church; in the lower part of the representation we can make out a colonnade incorporating a portico, with an attic above pierced by windows and a group of three domes that dominates the whole complex. The inscription exactly repeats that of the first coin: " REDEMPTORI VOTUM MDLXXVI." [7]

The other two unique pieces also offer new variations. They retain the ducal inscription on the reverse, except for the citation of the year of the dogate; however, the inscription is no longer placed in the center but around the edge, and the center is left free to contain the architectural representation. In the first coin, the building is octagonal (Fig. XIX, p. 58), rising on a high stylobate reached from all sides by three steps; the structure is surmounted by a dome crowned by a lantern.[8] The building in the second coin has a hexastyle portico (Fig. XXII, p. 60), with statues placed at the corners of the pediment and a wide flight of steps leading to the platform from which the columns rise.[9] The inscription on the reverse is identical in both coins: " REDEMPTORI VOTUM. "

The fact that several examples of the coin with the Lion of St. Mark on the pediment of the structure represented are preserved,[10] as well as the fact that the typical elements of the two sides of an *osella* are fused on the obverse, suggests that this coin was the actual celebratory piece destined by the doge for public distribution in 1576. According to Werdnig, the other four *oselle* — known only in single examples — should be recognized as rejected experimental models.[11] It is necessary to examine the annually-repeated arrangements for minting the *oselle* in order to disprove this hypothesis. The passages cited by Werdnig, which are taken from the *Cerimoniali ordinati per la Repubblica di Venezia e compilati da Giuseppe Ferrari, Cavaliere del doge Lod. Manin*,[12] inform us to some extent concerning the preparations for distributing the coins: G. Ferrari recounts how at the end of November, after the " Cassier delle Rason Vecchi " had earlier examined " alcuni disegni del impronto da farsi all'oselle," the doge specified the day for the coins to be distributed.

Since the models obviously had to be presented to the doge a long while in advance, we can guess that in 1576 this had been done before the November 17th and 22nd meetings of the Senate, which were dedicated to a definitive choice of the site for the votive church; this means that the models must have been presented when no one could yet have had a concrete idea of what the future church would look like.

The building on the reverse of the 1576 *osella* which survives in many examples is not attributable to any Venetian architect of the eighth decade of the Cinquecento, but instead closely recalls architectural efforts of the Early Renaissance in Venice; this confirms the fact that the representation cannot, in fact, be the reproduction of an actual plan, but must be the purely imaginative invention of a medalist. On the other hand, the four *oselle* known in single examples represent buildings stylistically typical of the last quarter of the century, which could certainly reproduce works either already constructed or projected. Certain details evident in the church as it was later built, as well as the definite resemblance of the coin representing the triple-domed church to an engraving in Rusconi's treatise, confirm this.[13] Since

the composition and the quality of the execution of the last four *oselle* is far superior to that of the *osella* destined for distribution, it is impossible to consider the four single pieces as experimental models which were later discarded. Moreover, the usual arrangement for selecting the design and minting the coins suggests that they cannot date later than the first few days of December 1576. Probably the four images on the reverses of the single pieces reproduce projects for the various sites under consideration for the church, elaborated during the period of the preliminary work and revealed during the Senate's sittings of the 17th and 22nd of November. The *terminus post quem*, which would be the date of the definitive choice of the site, is indicated by the observe of one of the coins showing the doge kneeling on the bank of the Giudecca.

The close analogy of one of the images to the church as it was eventually built demonstrates that the coin must reproduce a model executed after the plan. Since the decisions concerning the form that the new building was to assume were only made in February, all the projects that were presented had the same possibility of success at the time the four single pieces were coined; therefore, if one of these models was to be used as the pattern for a coin, at that moment it would have been possible to choose any of them, since any one of the projects could have been chosen for the votive church. But the *oselle* which were to be distributed had to be ready at the end of November;[14] thus it may possibly have been proposed that the 1576 series of *oselle* dedicated to the Republic's vow be improved or completed by reproducing the projects under discussion for the votive church, minting single successive examples or a limited series of celebratory coins of which only the best known examples are preserved.[15] These coins would have reproduced an imaginary design that would have had no real connection with the church being constructed. It is difficult to guess whether the " oselle straordinarie " subsequently minted were meant only for particular persons, such as private citizens who had donated money for the church's construction, or whether they were distributed to the top dignitaries, or whether they were specially commissioned by those who received them. Their superior state of preservation — especially the two with the centrally-planned churches — in comparison to that of the " oselle in serie " of the same year, suggests that they were not used as circulating money. In any case, in the history of the Redentore's construction they show that various projects, probably submitted by different architects, were certainly available quite early.

NOTES TO APPENDIX II

[1] Cf. BOERIO, 1829.

[2] This custom goes back to the doge's obligation to offer gifts to the nobility each year at Christmas. Originally game — especially royal mallards from the doge's hunting reserves — was distributed on this occasion. Eventually these gifts were replaced by a sum of money, and finally — in 1521 — by a silver coin equivalent to that sum which was minted annually for the purpose. Cf. WERDNIG, 1889.

[3] Cf. the decree of January 11, 1541. Archivio di Stato, Venice - *Cons.* X, *communi* F. 30.

[4] WERDNIG, 1889, p. 8.

[5] WERDNIG, 1889, pp. 55 ff.

[6] The *osella* is in the Museo Correr in Venice.

[7] The *osella* is in the British Museum in London.

[8] The *osella* is in the Museo Correr in Venice.

[9] The *osella* is in the British Museum in London.

[10] Some examples are in the Museo Correr, others are in the city museums of Vicenza, Bassano, Udine, etc.

[11] DA PORTOGRUARO, 1930, p. 162, suggests that these coins are commemorative medals deposited at the laying of the first stone of the church's foundations. But since this ceremony took place May 3, 1577, that date (and not 1576) would have had to appear on the coins. Moreover, we must bear in mind that commemorative medals portraying different buildings would not have been placed in the foundations of a definitively planned structure. Both the engraved images and the form of the inscriptions show that we are dealing here with *oselle* and not with commemorative medals.

[12] WERDNIG, 1889, pp. 3-7.

[13] 1660 (first ed. 1590), Bk. III, p. 61.

[14] PALATIO, 1696, reproduces all the *oselle* that previous doges had minted. For the year 1576 he publishes only the coin indicated here as the one intended for distribution, which he amply describes; on the other hand, he does not mention the four single examples.

[15] CORNELIO, 1749, records the text of another inscription on a coin that he saw in the famous Gradenigo collection: ERECTIONEM VOTIVI TEMPLI REFERT CHRISTO REDEMPTORI, ANNUMQUE EXHIBIT MDLXXVI. The form of the inscription, however, suggests that the coin was not an *osella*.

Chiosa del Redentore di Capuzini

I Procuratori di S. Marcho, cosi detti dalla cura et amministracione che hanno dell'entrate di quell'augustiss.º Tempio uestono perpetuamente la toga, essendo q.ta dignita suprema nella Republica.

Franco Forma con Priuilegio

XXIII - GIACOMO FRANCO, *A procurator of S. Mark's.* From *Habiti d'Huomeni et Donne Venetiane*, 1610

APPENDIX III

This appendix presents transcriptions of some of the more important documents for the history of the Redentore's construction, in order to help clarify the historical background of the vow that provided a conceptual unity underlying the church's design.

No. 1

Deliberatione del Senato di far voto alla Maestà Divina di fabricar in questa Città una Chiesa intitolata il Redentore per occasione della peste, con spender ducati diecimila.[1]

MDLXXVI. IV. Settembre in Pregadi.

Da quello che si legge, così nella Sacra Scrittura, come nell'historie delle cose passate, si conosse chiaramente, che quando la Maestà d'Iddio flagella pubblicamente un popolo, non si placa prima, che non sia publicamente con ogni segno d'humiltà supplicata: onde affligendo al presente questa città col flagello della peste è molto ben conveniente, che oltre, quanto è stato per il passato, si continui a ricorrer all'infinita sua clementia per impetrar misericordia pubblicamente, et con ogni devotione; Pero — L'Andera parte, che il Serenissimo Principe nostro, con li magistrati, et tutti li altri di questo conseglio con le veste che portano ordinariamente debbano andar li giorni prossimi di Zuoba, Venero, et Sabato nella chiesa nostra di San Marco, dove doppò udita la messa sia fatta ogni giorno processione, portando il santissimo sacramento, et pregando sua Divina Maestà per la liberatione di questa città dal presente flagello, et il sabbato giorno di nostra donna finita la processione, debba il Serenissimo Principe per nome publico far voto a sua Maestà, che si edificherà una chiesa a laude, et gloria sua intitolata al Redentor Nostro et che ogn'anno nel giorno, che questa città sara publicata libera dal presente contagio, sua Serenità et li successori suoi andera solennemente a visitar la predetta chiesa, a perpetua memoria del beneficio ricevuto. Et da mo sia preso, che per la edificatione della detta chiesa, la qual debba esser fabricata in quel luogo, che parerà a questo conseglio, sia speso fino alle summa de diesi mille et siano eletti dai nobili nostri del corpo di questo conseglio per scrutinio di esso, i quali habbino carico di far edificar essa chiesa con quella spesa, che sara conveniente, non facendo in essa lavori ne mettendovi pietre di marmo: ma facendo una fabrica soda, et quale si conviene ad una devota chiesa; nella qual siano deputati due capellani che habbino ad officiarla continuamente da esser eletti per il collegio nostro di tempo in tempo, con assignatione de ducati sessanta all'anno per cadauno delli danari della Signoria Nostra, fino, che sera loro provisto d'altro.

Da parte 84
De Non 2
Non sinc. 1

No. 2

L'Ordine, che fu tenuto nell'andar in chiesa per dar esecuzione al voto sopradetto.

MDLXXVI. Adi VIII. Settembre.[2]

Volendo il Serenissimo Principe Domino Alvise Mocenigo dare esecuzione al voto sudetto, fece publicar nel senato, che ogn'uno di esso venisse ad accompagnar sua Serenità con le vesti, che portava ordinariamente, li tre giorni, Giobia, Venere, et Sabato da matina prossimi sussequenti, per andar nella chiesa di San Marco per l'effetto suddetto; la quale il primo giorno di Giobbia, che fu alli sei Settembre accompagnata dal Senato, dalli magistrati maggiori, et anco da quelli del collegio tutto (caminando però con l'ordine che si tiene nelle altre processioni) dal Reverendo Primicerio, et suoi clerici, et altri della corte, secondo 'l solito suo ordine si condusse nel mezo di essa chiesa, il quale era serrato in quadro da diverse banche, nel capo delle quali alla mano destra era posta la sedia di sua Serenità nella sinistra una catthedra in disparte dalle sudette banche, sopra la qual sedeva il detto Reverendo Primicerio circondato da suoi clerici, et cantori, che stavano in piedi non molto lontano dall'Altare, che era preparato in faccia di questo loco, dove sono li gradi, per li quali si ascende nell'ingresso di mezo del choro con la santissima Eucharestia di sopra; sedendo tutti gli altri in esse banche con il solito suo ordine. Furno cominciate le lettanie musicalmente a due chori, et levatosi ogn'uno, quando fu tempo, andò a far la processione con quello istesso ordine, co'l quale s'era entrato nella detta chiesa, portando sotto l'ombrella la sacratissima Eucharestia Sopradetta; la qual ombrella era medessimamente portata dalli Sauij di Terra ferma, honorata da molti lumi, et da quelli, che ciascuno portava in mano co'l capo discoperto. Fatta detta processione et finite esse lettanie, fu detta la messa picciola; la qual finita sua Serenità se ne ritornò nel Palazzo, licentiando quelli che lo havevano accompagnato secondo'l consueto.

Fecessi il medesimo il secondo giorno di Venere, che fu alli sette, portandosi pero nella processione in luogo del santissimo sacramento un devotissimo Crocifisso di forma grande et cosi Sabbato il terzo giorno, che fu alli otto, portandosi in luogo del sudetto Crocifisso la imagine di nostra donna la quale è stata dipinta di mano dello Evangelista Messer San Luca, custodita gia gran tempo con molta veneratione, et devotione di tutta la città nel sacrario della detta Chiesa di San Marco. Ma innanzi che fusse celebrata la messa, il Serenissimo Principe sopradetto levatosi in piedi co'l corno in mano, et con la sua solita gravità, et prudentia parlò in questa sostanza.

Che affligendo il Signor Dio li populi per li peccati commesse contra sua Divina Maestà si come si deve credere, che faccia hora questa città, et leggersi nelle sacre scritture di haver fatto per li peccati commessi dal Re David nel populo Israelitico, facendone morir una gran parte di esso et non volendo prima placarsi, che fusse pregato da esso Re David a convertire il suo giusto flagello in se medesimo, che haveva peccato; et insieme honorato, et adorato publicamente sopra l'altar eretto da lui per conseglio di Gad Profeta; essortava sua Serenità pero ogn'uno col tal esempio a far penitenza dei suoi peccati, et con puro core convertirsi a dimandar perdono al Signor Dio, lo qual humilmente supplicava a perdonar a questo populo, et a voler comandar all'Agnello percutiente, che hormai cessasse la mano sua da tanta mortalità; et con l'istesso esempio del Re David sudetto (le parole del quale si stimava sua Serenità indegna di dover dire) che convertisse in se medesimo questo flagello, per espiation della sua giusta ira, prometteva di erigger per publico decreto una chiesa, intitolandola dal nome del REDENTORE con obligo per se, et suoi successori di visitarla in quello istesso giorno, nel qual saria sta dechiarito et publicato questa città libera dal contagio presente. Qui finito il suo ragionamento si cominciò la messa, la qual fù cantata musicalmente, et solennemente celebrata. Ritornando sua Serenità nel Palazzo fù ogn'uno licentiato secondo l'ordinario.

No. 3

(MDLXXVI. Settembre)
Di XVIII Detto [3]

Dovendosi dar essecutione al Voto fatto al Signor Dio per deliberatione di questo Consiglio intorno la Chiesa, che si deve eriger al Redentor nostro; Et essendo deliberato, che per esso Consiglio sia fatta elettione del loco, che si doverà trovar per questo effetto, e ben trovar modo, che havuta buona informatione si possi più facilmente deliberer quello, che sarà giudicato meglio, però

L'anderà parte, che de presenti per scrutinio di questo Consiglio sia fatta elettione di due Nobili nostri del corpo di esso, con titolo di Proveditori sopra la fabricha di essa Chiesa, potendo esser tolti di ogni luogo officio, conseglio, et anco officio continuo, et con pena, non potendo però per questa elettione lasciar li altri carichi, che avessero, overo che potessero haverli quali debbano andar vedendo per tutta la città li luoghi, che saranno giudicati oportuni per questo effetto, et siano tenuti in termine de giorni Tre prossimi venir à far relatione nel Collegio nostro di tutti li luoghi, che haveranno veduti; Et intesa la relatione loro, siano tenuti tutti quelli di esso collegio insieme con li detti Proveditori venir a questo Consiglio uniti, ò separati, à metter quelle parti, che loro pareranno, accio che il predetto Consiglio possi fare elettione di quel luogo, che stimerà più à proposito, et poi caminar inanzi alla edificatione di essa Chiesa.

. . . .	74	Electi illico per scrutinio in Consiglio.
. . . . . .	3	Rogator.
. . . . . .	2	S. Augustinus Barbarigo fo. de . . . . S. Lorenzo. S. Antonius Bragadeno fo. de . . . . S. Andrea.

No. 4

(MDLXXVI. Novembre) [4]
Di XXII detto

Volemo, che la Chiesa sia fabricata nel loco della Zudeca apresso li capuzzini, et officiata da loro, et sia tolto, XVI passa di Terreno per larghezza sopra la fondamenta, continuando à quella medesima larghezza fino à passa 40 per longhezza, con l'esborsatione de ducati Tremille alli patroni del fondo, sicome si sono contentati.

. . . . . .	68	Il Serenissimo Principe subito presa la soprascritta parte si levò in piedi, et premosse alcune parole con molto affetto, offeri per la Fabricha di detta chiesa ducati Mille cinquecento.

Populi frequentia nocturna, et exultatio prope Ecclesiam S̄s̄m̄i Redemptoris in Judaica ejusdem contingente pervigilio
Apud Ludovicum Furlanetto supra Pontem, vulgo dictum dei Baretteri C.P.E.S.

XXIV - GIAN BATTISTA BRUSTOLON, *The Festa del Redentore.*
From a painting by Canaletto

No. 5 [5]

(MDLXXVI. Febraro)
Di IX Detto

Dovendo si segondo il voto fatto dalla Signoria Nostra à 4 settembre passato edificar à laude et gloria di sua divina Maestà la Chiesa intitolata al Redentor nostro al luogo delli Capuzzini alla Zudeca, siccome è stato similmente preso in questo Consiglio a 22 di Novembre passato, però

L'andera parte, che sia commesso alli Provveditori, che debbano far principiar essa chiesa in forma quadrangular, sicome meglio parera alla maggior parte del Collegio nostro con intervento, et ballottation delli detti Provveditori: Nella qual fabrica non si possa spender, oltre il fondo, et li donativi fatti, più de ducati dieci, fin dodeci mille di danari della Signoria Nostra. Dovendosi osservar anco in materia di detta fabrica quanto si contiene in essa deliberatione di detto Conseglio di 4 di settembre passato.

. . . . 103

No. 6

Ordine del Collegio con l'auttorità del Senato, che detta chiesa sia fatta secondo il modello presentato in Collegio.

MDLXXVI. a XVII di Febraro in Collegio con intervento, et ballotation di Provveditori sopra la chiesa, et auttorità del Senato. [6]

Havendo li Provveditori sopra la chiesa presentato in questo Collegio un dissegno, formato dal fedel nostro Andrea Palladio in forma quadrangulare, et sopra esso fatto veder, che per i calcali diligentemente fatti dal detto Palladio, et dal fedel Antonio dal Ponte proto, non si spenderà nella fabricà più de ducati dodecimille dei danari della Signoria nostra, oltre l'amontar del fondo, et donativi giusta la parte del Senato dei IX del mese presente. Sia per auttorità di questo Collegio approbato esso dissegno, et secondo quello dato principio col nome del Spirito Santo al fabricar della detta Chiesa.

Ordine del Collegio con l'auttorità del Senato, che siano tolti altri passa quatro di larghezza, et quaranta di longhezza per far maggior la chiesa votata.

MDLXXVI. a XVIII Febraro in Collegio con l'intervento et ballotation di Proveditori, **sopra la chiesa, et auttorità del Senato.**

Essendo troppo angusto il luogo delli XVI passa di larghezza tolto nel terren delli Nobili nostri Lippomani alla Zudecca appresso i capucini, dove si ha da fabricare la chiesa pubblica sia per auttorità di questo Collegio preso, che sian tolti dalli detti Nobili nostri altri quatro passa di larghezza, et quaranta di longhezza per dar con questo aggionta la debita portione alla detta chiesa, et alle stradelle d'intorno, cosi consigliando i Proveditori di essa, et siano pagati essi quatro passa di larghezza, et quaranta di longhezza a rata portione delli passa XVI di larghezza et quaranta di longhezza, comprati da loro per deliberation del Senato per ducati tremille.

No. 7

Ordine tenuto nel metter la prima pietra nella chiesa votata. MDLXXVII a di III Mazo.[7]

Havendosi ragionato, nell'eccellentissimo Collegio et posto ordine di metter la prima pietra della chiesa del voto fatto per occasion della peste il Serenissimo Principe accompagnato da tutto detto eccellentissimo Collegio cioè Signori Consiglieri vestiti di scarlato, capi di Quaranta, et Sauij di tutte tre le mano di paonazzo, et li Auogadori, Capi dell'Illustrissimo Consiglio di X, et censori di scarlato secondo l'ordinario et sua sublimità è con veste Ducale di raso cremesino, si conferi pocco dopo terza alla Zudecha, et udi la messa nella Chiesa della croce, dove era la solennità, essendo quel giorno dell'inventione della Santissima Croce del Redentor nostro, et fò di Venere, chiesa più vicina d'ogn'altra al convento delli padri capuzzini, dove si haveva da fondar la predetta chiesa votiva, et mentre si cantò la messa; il Reverendissimo Patriarcha di Venetia, che prima era andato sopra il luogo a far l'officio, et cerimonie per la fondatione della chiesa, attese alle dette cerimonie a benedittione di detto luogo, al quale finita la messa, si conferi anco sua sublimità con tutti li soprascritti Eccellentissimi Signori et con li preti, et cantori di San Marco, havendo anco fatto condur due pietre per poner nelle fondamente, si che all'arrivo di sua Sublimità la quale stete presente a questo effetto, esso Reverendissimo Patriarcha andò lui medesimo a far metter dette pietre, quali furono poste una sopra l'altra in piano nella fondamenta, et sopra di esse erano descritte le parole sottoscritte; le qual pietre erano die longhezza die piedi.... et larghezza di piedi.

Redemptori Deo sancto dicatum. Ex pio solemniq. Reipublicae voto, ad arcenda fulgura dirae pestis. Gregorio XIII Pontifice Maxime Aloysio Mo-

cenigo Venetiarum Duce Johanne Triuisano Patriarcha Venetiarum M.D.LXXVI Die tertia Maij.[8]

Et poste le ditte pietre nelle fondamente, et havendo esso Reverendissimo Patriarca benedetto tutto'l luogo, dove va la fondamenta di detta chiesia con le orationi consuete, si parti sua Sublimità et sua Signoria Reverendissima et nel detto giorno si chiamò il gran Consiglio.

No. 8

Cerimonia fatta nel Publicar la Città libera dal contagio.[9]

M.D.LXXVII a XIII di Luglio in **Pregadi.**

Essendo passati molti giorni, che per gratia del Sommo Iddio non è morto, ne ferito alcuno da mal contagioso in questa Città nostra, si che'l lazareto vecchio pur per gratia di Santa Divina Maestà si attrova del tutto netto. Ne dovendosi per render primemente le debite gratie al Salvator nostro, era publico beneficio, et consolatione universale tardar più a publicar sana, et libera da contagio essa Città nostra; Però

L'andera parte, che co'l nome del Spirito Santo si debba fare la cerimonia della predetta publicatione la terza Dominica del mese presente. Et nella Chiesa nostra di San Marco si debba in detto giorno celebrar una solenne messa la qual udita dal Serenissimo Principe nostro dalli Magistrati, et da tutti li altri del Senato si debba con solenne processione andar poi a visitar la chiesa votiva intitolata al Redentor nostro si come ogn'anno ancora in tal giorno della terza Dominica del presente mese di Luglio dovera Sua Serenità et li suoi Successori andar solennemente alla predetta Chiesa a perpetua memoria del singolar beneficio ricevuto, si come è stato preso in detto Consiglio per il voto fatto a IIII di settembre prossimamente passato.

No. 9

Ponte fatto dalle colonne di San Marco fino alla Zudeca per visitar la chiesa votiva.

M.D.LXXVII a di XI Luglio in giorno di Dominica.[10]

Essendo stato fatto un ponte sopra galee, barchi, et piate, quale passava dalle colonne di San Marco fino a San Zuanne della Zudecha, ed essendo prima sta datto ordine, che le scole grandi, congregationi di frati, et preti venissero tutti alla processione; il Serenissimo Principe venne in Chiesa di San Marco vestito con manto d'arzento, accompagnato dalli Ambasciatori di Francia, Savoglia, et Ferrara all'hora ressidenti in questa Città, et dalli Signori Consiglieri, Capi di quaranta Procuratori, et da tutti quelli del Senato, li quali tutti cosi quelli, che mettono come quelli, che non mettono ballota in detto Senato, furono invitati il giorno avanti nel Senato sopradetto alla detta processione, et vennero con veste de seda, et cantata una solennissima messa dal Reverendissimo Patriarcha di Venetia, il quale dapoi ditte molte parole latine per il Primicerio di castello ringratiando sua divina Maestà che si era degnata di liberer questa città da tanto flagello, diede la benedittione, et poi per Zan Carlo Scaramella Nodaro della Cancelleria Ducale fò recitata una oratione pur in lingua latina nell'istesso proposito. Cominciò poi, et continuò a caminar la processione da San Marco passando per il ponte, fatto nel modo soprascritto fino al luogo di Scapuzini, dove già è fatta buona parte della fondamenta della Chiesa, che si deve fabricar in detto luogo, et era preparato un'altare eminente, a fine, che nel passar della processione, le genti facessero riverentia, et oratione per ditta liberatione; all'incontro del qual altare era preparato un luogo in forma di Teatro con una sedia per sua Sublimità et con banche adornate per la Serenissima Signoria et altri Senatori.

Le scole grandi, che furono le prime secondo l'ordinario, fecero tutte belissimo aparato con molti argenti, et tutte con grandissimo numero di fratelli di ditte scole. Et tra le altre quella di San Todaro hebbe gran..... d'argenti: ma superò di gran l'onga quella di San Rocho la quale oltra grandissima quantità d'argenti sopra solari, et portati da diversi bastasi fece anco pur sopra solari diverse dimostrationi et Figure, cosa honoratissima da vedere sicome fò anco a veder il molto populo, che concorse a questa devotione, essendo stata si può dir tutta la città. Dietro il Clero, che è sempre l'ultimo in le processioni, et il capitolo di Castello andorono li comandadori, et poi seguiva la croce del capitolo di San Marco con li preti del coro, et cantori, et la nostra donna con sie torze avanti, et sie dopoi portate da quelli laici, che per avanti le havevano portate nelle processioni, che si fecero ogni giorno. Seguivano poi li canonici, con piviali, et il Primicerio di San Marco, con rochetto in mezo di doi canonici. Venivano poi li ministri del Reverendissimo Patriarcha di Venetia con piviali, et.... sua Signoria Reverendissima vestita in Pontificale, dietro il quale venivano li scudieri, gastaldi, secretarij et altri secondo l'ordinario.

No. 10

La liberatione di Vinegia.[11]

Al molto Magnifico et eccellentissimo Signore, Signor G. F.

Sapra adunque Vostra Magnificenza che del 1575 a' 21 di Luglio cominciò la peste in Vinegia, e molte case hanno patito infettione. Alli 4 Settembre poi 1576 essendo in colmo morire, questi Christianissimi Padri fecero unitamente Voto di edificar una Chiesa a' Reverendi Padri Capuccini alla Giudeca dedicandola al Sommo Nostro Redentore perche cessasse cosi horrendo male. Hora cessata del tutto miracolosamente la peste, memori del beneficio recevuto da Sua Divina Maiestà presero parte nell'Illustrissimo Senato di pubblicar la liberatione della Città al li 21 Luglio 1577 (che a questo modo ha durato la peste due anni giusti) e visitar la Chiesa votiva solennemente, nel modo, e ordine, che vi scriverò con quella brevità, che si potrà: e questa visitatione solenne la faranno ogn'anno.

Dovete avertire, che la Chiesa visitata non è quasi principiata ma si come tutte l'altre cose sono state fatte con gran celerità, cosi quel luogo pieno delle rovinate habitationi, che già v'erano, è stato in tal maniera disposto, che né rivene, né mal composti pavimenti hanno dato noia alcuna. Era fatto una porta a detta Chiesa coperta maestrevolmente di minutissime foglie d'alberi levata da' tronconi, dentro dalla quale vi era una assai lunga strada coperta di panni fini di molto prezzo, dalla quale si giungea in un spacioso Choro acconcio gratiosamente, e addobbato di cuoi d'oro, e razzi finissimi nel mezo del quale era su per molti gradi un'altare, eminente con l'imagine del Nostro Redentore fatta da dottissima mano, ornato d'illustri spalliere d'oro, di seda e d'archento. Serviano quivi al Sommo Dio li Reverendi Padri Capuccini.

Discendendo poi giù per l'altra parte dell'altare si venia ad un'altra strada, come la prima coperta, per laquale si giungea ad un'altra porta fatta come quell'altra di foglie, per laqual fu il ritorno. Sarà questa Chiesa capace, e bella. V'ho detto prima della Chiesa, perche parlandosi molto d'essa si sappia in che termine sta....

. . . . 1577
Di Vinegia alli 22. Luglio   Affettionatiss. servitore
D.V.M.   Mutio Lumina

No. 11

Cerimonia usata da sua Serenità nell'andar a visitar la chiesa votiva del Redentore.[12]

M.D.LXXVIII a di XX Luglio.

In essecution di quanto fu deliberato nel Eccellentissimo Consiglio di Pregadi a 13 luglio 1577 in proposito dell'andar il Serenissimo Principe a visitar la chiesa votiva; questa matina la Serenità sua accompagnata dalli Ambasciatori di Francia et Savogia, Consiglieri Capi di quaranta Procuratori et da tutto il Senato, cosi da quelli, che mettono, come da quelli, che non mettono balotte vestita con manto d'Argento, se ne è andata nella sudetta chiesa. Furono li soprascritti del Senato invitati tutti et dettoli, che ognuno dovesse andar vestito di seda, et che quelli di essi, che per la incapacità delli piati non havessero havuto luoco in essi, se ne fossero andati nelle loro gondole, si come fu fatto. Prima, che sua Serenità si sia partita di Palazzo ha udito la messa ordinaria di Collegio et un'altra cantata in Chiesa di San Marco, sono passati per Choro processionalmente tutti li preti, frati et scole di questa città li quali tutti se ne sono andati per terra alla sudetta chiesia, essendosi per ciò, et per commodità della città stati fatto doi ponti, l'uno a Santa Maria Zubenigo, et l'altro all'hospetal dello Spirito Santo, se bene l'anno passato ne fu fatto un solo della piazza fino a San Zuane della Zudeca.

NOTES TO APPENDIX III

[1] The text was extracted from *Cerimoniali* I, fol. xlvii v. Archivio di Stato, Venice.

[2] Archivio di Stato, Venice - *Cerimoniali* I, fol. xlviii r.

[3] Archivio di Stato, Venice - *Senato Terra*, R. 51, fol. 114 r.

[4] Archivio di Stato, Venice - *Senato Terra*, R. 51, fol. 134 r.

[5] Archivio di Stato, Venice - *Senato Terra*, R. 51, fol. 155 v. According to the official Venetian calculation the year began March 1st; therefore the date should actually read February 9, 1577.

[6] Archivio di Stato, Venice - *Cerimoniali* I, fol. l. This date is also " Venetian " and should therefore read 1577.

[7] Archivio di Stato, Venice - *Cerimoniali* I, fol. li r.

[8] This is an error in copying; one should read 1577 for 1576.

[9] Archivio di Stato, Venice - *Cerimoniali* I, fol. lix v.

[10] Archivio di Stato, Venice - *Cerimoniali* I, fol. lx. An error slipped by the copyist here, too: instead of " xi Luglio " one should read " xxi Luglio. "

[11] The text was copied from an example in the Biblioteca Marciana (Misc. 2380-21). Only the first part of the letter is quoted, in which the plan selected for the church and the temporary structure which had been erected on the site are described.

[12] Archivio di Stato, Venice - *Cerimoniali* I, fol. lxx v.

BIBLIOGRAPHY

1562 S. Serlio, *Il terzo libro di Sebastiano Serlio Bolognese nel quale si figurano e descrivono le antiquità di Roma, e le altre che sono in Italia e fuori d'Italia*, Venice.

G. Zarlino, *Le istituzioni harmoniche dal Reverendo M. Gioseffo Zarlino da Chioggia*, Venice.

1570 A. Palladio, *I Quattro Libri dell'Architettura*, Venice.

1577 M. Lumina, *La Liberatione di Vinegia*, n. p.

1604 J. Sansovino-G. Stringa, *Venetia città nobilissima et singolare. Descritta già in XIIII libri da M. Francesco Sansovino, et hora con molta diligenza corretta, emendata, e più d'un terzo di cose nuove ampliata dal M.R.D. Giovanni Stringa, Canonico della Chiesa Ducale di S. Marco*, Venice.

1610 G. Franco, *Habiti d'Huomeni et Donne Venetiane, con la Prozessione della serenissima Signoria et altri particolari, cioè Trionfi Feste et Ceremonie Publiche della Nobilissima Città di Venezia*, Venice.

1648 C. Ridolfi, *Le meraviglie dell'arte, overo le vite de gl'illustri pittori veneti e dello stato*, Venice (cf. also ed. D. F. von Hadeln, Berlin, 1914).

1660 G. A. Rusconi, *I dieci libri d'Architettura*, Venice.

1663 F. Sansovino, *Venetia città nobilissima et singolare. Descritta in XIIII libri da M. Francesco Sansovino, con aggiunte da D. Giustiniano Martinioni*, Venice.

1696 J. Palatio, *Fasti Ducales ab Anafesto I. al Silvestrum Valerium, Venetorum Ducem, cum eorum Iconibus, Insignibus, Nummismatibus Publicis et Privatis aere Sculptis. Studio Joannis Palatii*, Venice.

1703 L. Carlevaris, *Le fabriche e vedute di Venetia, disegnate, poste in prospettiva, et intagliate da Luca Carlevariis*, Venice.

1738 ff. T. Temanza, *Zibaldon* (ed. Nicola Ivanoff, Venice, 1963).

1740 *Forestiere illuminato intorno le cose più rare, e curiose, antiche e moderne della città di Venezia*, Venice.

1740-60 F. Muttoni, *Architettura di Andrea Palladio vicentino di nuovo ristampata con le osservazioni dell'Architetto N.N.*, Venice.

1749 F. Cornelio, *Ecclesiae Venetae antiquis monumentis, nunc etiam primum editis illustratae. Ac in Decades distributae Auctore Flaminio Cornelio senatore veneto*, Venice.

1762 T. Temanza, *Vita di Andrea Palladio vicentino egregio architetto*, Venice.

1786 J. W. von Goethe, *Italienische Reise* (ed. Herbert von Einem, Hamburg, 1951).

1796 O. Bertotti-Scamozzi, *Le fabbriche e i disegni di Andrea Palladio*, Vicenza.

1797 O. Bertotti-Scamozzi, *Le terme dei romani disegnate da Andrea Palladio e ripubblicate con la giunta di alcune osservazioni*, Vicenza.

1822 M. G. Bottari, *Raccolta di lettere sulla pittura, scultura et architettura, pubblicata da M. Giò Bottari e continuata fino ai nostri giorni da Stefano Ticozzi*, Milan.

1829 G. Boerio, *Dizionario del Dialetto Veneziano*, Venice.

1845 A. Magrini, *Memorie intorno la vita e le opere di Andrea Palladio*, Padua.

1889 G. Werdnig, *Die Osellen oder Münz-Medaillen der Republik Venedig*, Vienna-Milan.

1926 G. Lorenzetti, *Venezia e il suo estuario*, Milan-Venice.

1930 D. M. Da Portogruaro, " Il tempio e il convento del Redentore," in *Rivista della Città di Venezia*, IX.

1936 G. Gronau, *Documenti artistici urbinati*, Florence.

1938 L. H. Heydenreich, " Gedanken über Michelozzo di Bartolomeo," in *Festschrift Wilhelm Pinder*, Leipzig.

H. Hoffmann, *Hochrenaissance, Manierismus, Frühbarock*. Zurich-Leipzig.

1943 B. Betto, " L'iconografia della chiesa dell'SS. Redentore in Venezia," in *Ateneo Veneto*, CXXXIV.

1948 R. Pane, *Andrea Palladio*, Turin.

1954 J. S. Ackerman, *The Cortile del Belvedere*, Vatican City.

V. Moschini, *Canaletto*, Milan.

1955 H. Siebenhüner, " S. Maria degli Angeli in Rom," in *Münchner Jahrbuch der Bildenden Künste*, s. 3, VI.

1956 O. Förster, *Bramante*, Vienna-Munich.

R. Pane, " Andrea Palladio e l' interpretazione della architettura rinascimentale," in *Venezia e l' Europa, Atti del XVIII Congresso Internazionale di Storia dell'Arte*, Venice.

1958 H. Sedlmayr, *Kunst und Wahrheit. Zur Theorie und Methode der Kunstgeschichte*, Hamburg.

G. G. Zorzi, *I disegni delle antichità di Andrea Palladio*, Venice.

1959-60 W. Timofiewitsch, " Ein unbekannter Kirchenentwurf Palladios," in *Arte Veneta*, XIII-XIV.

1961 F. Cessi, *Alessandro Vittoria architetto e stuccatore*, Trent.

E. Hubala, " L. B. Albertis Langhaus von Sant Andrea in Mantua," in *Festschrift Kurt Badt*, Berlin.

1962 R. Wittkower, *Architectural Principles in the Age of Humanism*, London (3rd rev. ed.; first ed. 1949).

1964 W. Timofiewitsch, " Genesi e struttura della chiesa del Rinascimento veneziano," in *Bollettino del Centro Internazionale di Studi di Architettura Andrea Palladio*, VI, pt. 2, Vicenza.

R. Zeitler, " Una lettera falsificata del Palladio, " in *Bollettino del Centro Internazionale di Studi di Architettura Andrea Palladio*, VI, pt. 2, Vicenza.

1965   E. Forssman, *Palladios Lehrgebäude*, Stockholm-Göteborg-Uppsala.

E. Hubala, *Reclams Kunstführer, Oberitalien-Ost*, Stuttgart.

S. Sinding-Larsen, " Palladio's Redentore, a Compromise in Composition," in *The Art Bulletin*, XLVII.

1966   J. S. Ackerman, *Palladio*, Harmondsworth.

H. Spielmann, *Andrea Palladio und die Antike*, Munich-Berlin.

1967   G. G. Zorzi, *Le chiese e i ponti di Andrea Palladio*, Vicenza.

N. Ivanoff, *Palladio*, Milan.

W. Timofiewitsch, *Die Sakrale Architektur Palladios*, Munich.

E. Riccomini, " Opere veneziane di Giuseppe Maria Mazza," in *Arte Veneta*, XXI.

INDEX OF PERSONS AND PLACES

Names of persons are in small capital letters; names of places are in italics.

ACKERMAN, JAMES, 50 (n. 65, n. 80)

BARBARIGO, AGOSTINO, 49 (n. 6, n. 13), 66
BARBARO, MARC'ANTONIO, 15
BASSANO, FRANCESCO, 54, 56 (n. 16, n. 20, n. 26)
Bassano
  Museo Civico, 63 (n. 10)
BERTOTTI-SCAMOZZI, OTTAVIO, 23, 24, 25, 39
BETTO, BIANCA, 49 (n. 25)
BRAGADIN, ANTONIO, 49 (n. 6, n. 13, n. 32)
BRAMANTE, DONATO, 42, 43
BUONARROTI, MICHELANGELO, 43

CALIARI, BENEDETTO, 56 (n. 17)
CALIARI, CARLO, 56 (n. 17)
CALIARI, GABRIELE, 56 (n. 17)
CALIARI, PAOLO, 56 (n. 17)
CAMPAGNA, GIROLAMO, 39, 53, 54
CANALETTO, ANTONIO, 53
CARLEVARIS, LUCA, 53
CESSI, FRANCESCO, 49 (n. 41)
CICOGNA, PASQUALE, 55
CONTARINI, ZORZI, 17
CORNELIO, FLAMINIO, 63 (n. 15)
CORTE, JOSSE DE, 53

DA PONTE, ANTONIO, 17, 67
DA PORTOGRUARO, DAVIDE, 49 (n. 29), 56 (n. 6, n. 9, n. 13, n. 25, n. 32), 63 (n. 11)
DA VICENZA, GIUSEPPE, 56 (n. 25)
DE' BARBARI, JACOPO, 18, 36, 49 (n. 9), 50 (n. 56)

EINEM, HERBERT VON, 56 (n. 23)

Fano
  Basilica, 50 (n. 65)
FERRARI, GIUSEPPE, 62
FORSSMAN, ERIK, 50 (n. 65), 51 (n. 98)
FÖRSTER, OTTO, 50 (n. 74)
FRANCO, GIACOMO, 50 (n. 50), 53, 56 (n. 3)
GOETHE, JOHANN WOLFGANG VON, 56 (n. 23, n. 33)
GORNIZAI, ZANDOMENICO, 53
GREGORIO XIII, Pope, 50 (n. 47), 68
GRIMANI, GIOVANNI, 49 (n. 32)
GRONAU, GIORGIO, 56 (n. 29)

HEYDENREICH, LUDWIG, 50 (n. 67)
HOFFMAN, HANS, 50 (n. 52)
HUBALA, ERICH, 50 (n. 53, n. 71)

IVANOFF, NICOLA, 50 (n. 59), 56 (n. 9, n. 31)

LE CURT, GIUSTO (v. Corte)
London
  British Museum, 63 (n. 7, n. 9)
LONGHENA, BALDASSARE, 50 (n. 50)
LORENZETTI, GIULIO, 53, 56 (n. 1, n. 5, n. 18, n. 21)
LUMINA, MUTIO, 35, 39, 69

MAGRINI, ANTONIO, 49 (n. 29), 50 (n. 45)

MANIN, LODOVICO, 62
Mantua
  Church of Sant'Andrea, 42
MARTINIONI, GIUSTINIANO, 53, 55
MAZOLENI, FRANCESCO, 54
MAZZA, GIUSEPPE MARIA, 56 (n. 30)
Milan
  Church of Santa Maria delle Grazie, 42
MOCENIGO, ALVISE, 13, 17, 49 (n. 26), 50 (n. 50), 55, 61, 65, 68
MOSCHINI, VITTORIO, 56 (n. 11)
MUTTONI, PIETRO, 55

PALATIO, GIOVANNI, 63 (n. 14)
Palestrina
  Temple of Fortuna Primigenia, 43
PALLUCCHINI, RODOLFO, 49 (n. 25)
PALMA, JACOPO IL GIOVANE, 54, 56 (n. 19)
PANE, ROBERTO, 46, 50 (n. 53, n. 79), 51 (n. 90, n. 91)
PERUZZI, BALDASSARE, 43
PIAZZA, PAOLO, 50 (n. 41), 54
PRIULI, LORENZO, 18, 55

RICCOMINI, EUGENIO, 56 (n. 30)
RIDOLFI, CARLO, 56 (n. 17)
Rome
  Basilica of Maxentius, 51 (n. 93)
  Baths of Agrippa, 47
  Baths of Diocletian, 41
  Church of the Gesù, 41, 42
  Church of San Biagio della Pagnotta, 42
  Church of San Celso, 42
  Church of Sant'Eligio degli Orefici, 43
  Pantheon, 43, 47, 48

Tempietto at San Pietro in Montorio, 42
Temple of Jove, 50 (n. 79)
« Temple of Minerva Medica »,
    50 (n. 79)
Rome (Vatican)
    Belvedere Court, 43
    St. Peter's, 42
RUER, TOMMASO, 56 (n. 9, n. 31)
RUSCONI, G. ANTONIO, 15, 49
    (n. 13), 62

SANTI, RAPHAEL, 41, 42
SCARAMELLA, ZAN CARLO, 69
SEDLMAYR, HANS, 49 (n. 1)
SFORZA, LODOVICO, 42
SIEBENHÜNER, HERBERT, 50 (n. 83)
SINDING-LARSEN, STAALE, 49 (n.22),
    50 (n. 63)
SPIELMANN, HEINZ, 50 (n. 83)
STRINGA, GIOVANNI, 38, 49 (n. 38,
    n. 41), 50 (n. 46, n. 60, n. 62),
    53, 54, 55, 56 (n. 2, n. 14, n. 28,
    n. 34)

TEMANZA, TOMMASO, 49 (n. 15),
    56 (n. 9)
TERILLI, FRANCESCO, 56 (n. 15)
TIMOFIEWITSCH, WLADIMIR, 50
    (n. 41, n. 73, n. 77, n. 78), 51
    (n. 92), 56 (n. 24)

TINTORETTO, JACOPO, 49 (n. 26), 54
Tivoli
    Temple of Hercules Victor, 43
Todi
    Church of Santa Maria della Consolazione, 14, 42
Trent
    Castello del Buonconsiglio, 36
TREVISANO, GIOVANNI, 55, 68

Udine
    Museo Civico, 63 (n. 10)

VAROTARI, ALESSANDRO, 49 (n. 25)
Venice
    Biblioteca Marciana, 70 (n. 11)
    Campo San Vitale, 13, 14, 15
    Chiesa dei Gesuati, 34, 39
    Church of Santa Croce della Giudecca, 14, 15
    Church of Santa Croce di Venezia, 14, 15, 49 (n. 9)
    Church of San Francesco della Vigna, 46
    Church of San Giorgio Maggiore,
        34, 38, 42, 43, 46, 47, 49
    (n. 24, n. 41), 56 (n. 28)
    Church of San Giovanni della
        Giudecca, 36, 50 (n. 56), 70

Church of Santa Maria della Salute, 50 (n. 50), 53
Church of Santa Maria delle Zitelle, 28
Church of Santa Maria Maggiore,
    49 (n. 13, n. 15)
Church of Santa Maria Zobenigo,
    36, 70
Doges' Palace, 43, 61
Museo Correr, 50 (n. 58), 63
    (n. 6, n. 8, n. 10)
Ospedale di Spirito Santo, 36, 70
Piazzetta di San Marco, 34, 61
St. Mark's, 13, 35, 65, 66, 68,
    70
VERONESE (v. Caliari)
Vicenza
    Museo Civico, 63 (n. 10)
    Palazzo Valmarana, 43
    Santuario di Monte Berico, 14
VITRUVIUS, 44

WERDNIG, GEORG, 62, 63 (n. 2,
    n. 4, n. 5, n. 12)
WITTKOWER, RUDOLF, 46, 50 (n.44,
    n. 68), 51 (n. 89, n. 96)

ZEITLER, RUDOLF, 49 (n. 39)
ZORZI, GIANGIORGIO, 49 (n. 2,
    n. 18), 50 (n. 66, n. 69, n. 70,
    n. 81, n. 82, n. 84), 51 (n. 95,
    n. 97)

ILLUSTRATIONS IN THE TEXT

I   ANDREA PALLADIO, *Chiesa del Redentore, front elevation.* From *Architettura di Andrea Palladio ... con le osservazioni dell'architetto N.N.,* Vol. IV, Venice, 1743

II   ANDREA PALLADIO, *Chiesa del Redentore, front elevation.* From *Le Fabbriche e i Disegni di Andrea Palladio raccolti e illustrati da Ottavio Bertotti Scamozzi,* Vol. IV, Vicenza, 1783

III   ANDREA PALLADIO, *Chiesa del Redentore, transverse section.* From *Architettura di Andrea Palladio ... con le osservazioni dell'architetto N.N.,* Vol. IV, Venice, 1743

IV   ANDREA PALLADIO, *Chiesa del Redentore, longitudinal section.* From *Le Fabbriche e i Disegni di Andrea Palladio raccolti e illustrati da Ottavio Bertotti Scamozzi,* Vol. IV, Vicenza, 1783

V   ANDREA PALLADIO, *Chiesa del Redentore, plan.* From *Architettura di Andrea Palladio ... con le osservazioni dell'architetto N.N.,* Vol. IV, Venice, 1743

VI   ANDREA PALLADIO, *Chiesa del Redentore, plan.* From *Le Fabbriche e i Disegni di Andrea Palladio raccolti e illustrati da Ottavio Bertotti Scamozzi,* Vol. IV, Vicenza, 1783

VII   ANDREA PALLADIO, *Baths of Agrippa, plan.* From *Le terme dei romani disegnate da Andrea Palladio,* by Ottavio Bertotti Scamozzi, Vicenza, 1797

VIII   ANDREA PALLADIO, *Chiesa del Redentore, left flank.* From *Architettura di Andrea Palladio ... con le osservazioni dell'architetto N.N.,* Vol. IV, Venice, 1743

IX   ANDREA PALLADIO, *Chiesa del Redentore, longitudinal section.* From *Architettura di Andrea Palladio ... con le osservazioni dell'architetto N.N.,* Vol. IV, Venice, 1743

X   ANDREA PALLADIO, *Chiesa del Redentore, plan and elevation of a side chapel.* From *Architettura di Andrea Palladio ... con le osservazioni dell'architetto N.N.,* Vol. IV, Venice, 1743

XI   ANDREA PALLADIO, *Baths of Diocletian, detail of elevation.* London, R.I.B.A., V/6

XII   ANDREA PALLADIO, *Baths of Titus, front elevation.* London, R.I.B.A., II/6

XIII   SEBASTIANO SERLIO, *plan of St. Peter's after Raphael.* From *Il Terzo Libro di Sebastiano Serlio Bolognese,* Venice, 1562

XIV   ANDREA PALLADIO, *design for a façade.* London, R.I.B.A., XIV/10

XV   ANDREA PALLADIO, *Baths of Diocletian, detail of a section.* London, R.I.B.A., V/2

XVI   DONATO BRAMANTE, *Tempietto at San Pietro in Montorio.* From *I Quattro Libri dell'Architettura di Andrea Palladio,* Bk. IV, Ch. 17, Venice, 1570

XVII   *Votive painting showing the doge Alvise Mocenigo* (formerly in the Robilant collection)

XVIII   *Osella of Doge Alvise Mocenigo for 1576.* Venice, Museo Correr

XIX   *Osella of Doge Alvise Mocenigo for 1576* (unique). Venice, Museo Correr

XX   *Osella of Doge Alvise Mocenigo for 1576* (unique). Venice, Museo Correr

XXI   *Osella of Doge Alvise Mocenigo for 1576* (unique). London, British Museum

XXII   *Osella of Doge Alvise Mocenigo for 1576* (unique). London, British Museum

XXIII   GIACOMO FRANCO, *A procurator of St. Mark's.* From *Habiti d'Huomeni et Donne Venetiane,* 1610

XXIV   GIAN BATTISTA BRUSTOLON, *The Festa del Redentore.* From a painting by Canaletto

PLATES

1   Venice. The Chiesa del Redentore in its setting on the Giudecca. Aerial view

2   Venice. The Chiesa del Redentore seen from the Zattere

3   Venice. The Chiesa del Redentore: front view

4   Chiesa del Redentore: façade seen from the piazzetta in front of the church

5   Chiesa del Redentore: detail of the façade

6   Chiesa del Redentore: detail of the façade showing a portion of the left flank

7   Chiesa del Redentore: detail of the façade

8   Chiesa del Redentore: detail of the façade

9   Chiesa del Redentore: detail of the façade

10   Chiesa del Redentore: detail of the façade

11   Chiesa del Redentore: detail of the façade

12   Chiesa del Redentore: niche at the left of the entrance portal; statue of St. Mark

13   Chiesa del Redentore: niche at the right of the entrance portal; statue of St. Francis

14   Chiesa del Redentore: composite capital of one of the half-columns on the façade

15   Chiesa del Redentore: composite capital of one of the façade pilasters

16   Chiesa del Redentore: apse seen from the priory garden

17   Chiesa del Redentore: right flank

18   Chiesa del Redentore: detail showing the pitch of the roof on the left side and some of the buttresses

19   Chiesa del Redentore: view of pilasters and buttresses along the left flank

20   Chiesa del Redentore: view of the wall of the monks' choir and one of the bell-towers flanking the dome

21   Chiesa del Redentore: detail of Plate 20

22   Chiesa del Redentore: interior seen from the entrance

23   Chiesa del Redentore: interior seen from the presbytery

24   Chiesa del Redentore: left side of the nave

25   Chiesa del Redentore: nave vault

26   Chiesa del Redentore: detail of the Corinthian order in the nave

27   Chiesa del Redentore: detail of the Corinthian order in the nave

28   Chiesa del Redentore: a side chapel of the nave

29   Chiesa del Redentore: detail of a side chapel

30   Chiesa del Redentore: detail of a side chapel

31   Chiesa del Redentore: detail of a side chapel

32   Chiesa del Redentore: detail of a side chapel

33   Chiesa del Redentore: corner of the nave, showing the steps to the presbytery

34   Chiesa del Redentore: left crossing apse

35   Chiesa del Redentore: left crossing apse

36   Chiesa del Redentore: beveled crossing pier

37   Chiesa del Redentore: presbytery; main altar and exedra

38   Chiesa del Redentore: left side of the presbytery seen from the drum of the dome

39   Chiesa del Redentore: exedra seen from the monks' choir

40   Chiesa del Redentore: vault of the exedra and part of the dome

41   Chiesa del Redentore: dome

42   Chiesa del Redentore: drum of the dome

43   Chiesa del Redentore: dome flanked by the vaults of the nave and apses

44   Chiesa del Redentore: detail of the Corinthian order in the presbytery

45   Chiesa del Redentore: detail of a crossing pier

46   Chiesa del Redentore: capital of a half-column and pilaster in one of the crossing piers

47   Chiesa del Redentore: capital of a half-column and pilaster in one of the crossing piers

48   Chiesa del Redentore: capital of a column of the exedra behind the main altar

49   Chiesa del Redentore: capital of a column of the exedra behind the main altar

50   Chiesa del Redentore: lower portion of the exedra columns, showing the entrance to the monks' choir

51   Chiesa del Redentore: bases of the exedra columns

52   Chiesa del Redentore: bases of the half-column of the entrance portal and the adjacent giant half-column of the façade

53   Chiesa del Redentore: bases of the half-columns in the nave

54   Chiesa del Redentore: monks' choir

55   Chiesa del Redentore: main altar

56   GIROLAMO CAMPAGNA, bronze crucifix on the main altar

57   Chiesa del Redentore: upper part of the tabernacle of the main altar, with bronze statues by GIUSEPPE MARIA MAZZA

58   TOMMASO RUER, *Christ Carrying the Cross.* Marble relief decorating the main altar

59   GIROLAMO CAMPAGNA, *St. Mark.* Bronze statue on the left side of the main altar

60   GIROLAMO CAMPAGNA, *St. Francis.* Bronze statue on the right side of the main altar

61   Chiesa del Redentore: pavement of the presbytery

62   Chiesa del Redentore: holy-water font at the left of the entrance

63   Chiesa del Redentore: holy-water font at the right of the entrance

64   FRANCESCO BASSANO, *The Nativity.* Altarpiece in the first chapel on the right

65   CARLO and GABRIELE CALIARI, *The Baptism of Christ.* Altarpiece in the second chapel on the right

66   School of JACOPO TINTORETTO, *The Flagellation.* Altarpiece in the third chapel on the right

67   PALMA IL GIOVANE, *The Entombment.* Altarpiece in the third chapel on the left

68   FRANCESCO BASSANO, *The Resurrection.* Altarpiece in the second chapel on the left

69   Workshop of JACOPO TINTORETTO, *The Ascension.* Altarpiece in the first chapel on the left

70   FRANCESCO BASSANO, *The Resurrection* (detail). Altarpiece in the second chapel on the left

COLOR PLATES

a)   The Chiesa del Redentore seen from the Zattere

b)   The Chiesa del Redentore, right flank

SCALE DRAWINGS

a - Chiesa del Redentore: plan

b - Chiesa del Redentore: façade elevation

c - Chiesa del Redentore: side elevation

d - Chiesa del Redentore: longitudinal section

e - Chiesa del Redentore: transverse section showing nave and crossing

f - Chiesa del Redentore: elevation and plan of a portion of the nave

g - Chiesa del Redentore: elevation of a chapel

h - Chiesa del Redentore: section of a chapel

THE SCALE DRAWINGS WERE EXECUTED BY DR. ARCH. GILDA D'AGARO IN
COLLABORATION WITH DR. ARCH. MARIA TARLÀ AND MARIO TOMASUTTI

PLATES

1 - Venice. The Chiesa del Redentore in its setting on the Giudecca. Aerial view

2 - Venice. The Chiesa del Redentore seen from the Zattere

3 - Venice. The Chiesa del Redentore: front view

4 - Chiesa del Redentore: façade seen from the piazzetta in front of the church

5 - Chiesa del Redentore: detail of the façade

6 - Chiesa del Redentore: detail of the façade showing a portion of the left flank

7 - Chiesa del Redentore: detail of the façade

8 - Chiesa del Redentore: detail of the façade

9 - Chiesa del Redentore: detail of the façade

10 - Chiesa del Redentore: detail of the façade

11 - Chiesa del Redentore: detail of the façade

12 - Chiesa del Redentore: niche at the left of the entrance portal; statue of St. Mark

13 - Chiesa del Redentore: niche at the right of the entrance portal; statue of St. Francis

14 - Chiesa del Redentore: composite capital of one of the half-columns on the façade

15 - Chiesa del Redentore: composite capital of one of the façade pilasters

16 - Chiesa del Redentore: apse seen from the priory garden

17 - Chiesa del Redentore: right flank

18 - Chiesa del Redentore: detail showing the pitch of the roof on the left side and some of the buttresses

19 - Chiesa del Redentore: view of pilasters and buttresses along the left flank

20 - Chiesa del Redentore: view of the wall of the monks' choir and one of the bell-towers flanking the dome

21 - Chiesa del Redentore: detail of Plate 20

22 - Chiesa del Redentore: interior seen from the entrance

23 - Chiesa del Redentore: interior seen from the presbytery

24 - Chiesa del Redentore: left side of the nave

25 - Chiesa del Redentore: nave vault

26 - Chiesa del Redentore: detail of the Corinthian order in the nave

27 - Chiesa del Redentore: detail of the Corinthian order in the nave

28 - Chiesa del Redentore: a side chapel of the nave

29 - Chiesa del Redentore: detail of a side chapel

30 - Chiesa del Redentore: detail of a side chapel

31 - Chiesa del Redentore: detail of a side chapel

32 - Chiesa del Redentore: detail of a side chapel

33 - Chiesa del Redentore: corner of the nave, showing the steps to the presbytery

34 - Chiesa del Redentore: left crossing apse

35 - Chiesa del Redentore: left crossing apse

36 - Chiesa del Redentore: beveled crossing pier

37 - Chiesa del Redentore: presbytery; main altar and exedra

38 - Chiesa del Redentore: left side of the presbytery seen from the drum of the dome

39 - Chiesa del Redentore: exedra seen from the monks' choir

40 - Chiesa del Redentore: vault of the exedra and part of the dome

41 - Chiesa del Redentore: dome

42 - Chiesa del Redentore: drum of the dome

43 - Chiesa del Redentore: dome flanked by the vaults of the nave and apses

44 - Chiesa del Redentore: detail of the Corinthian order in the presbytery

45 - Chiesa del Redentore: detail of a crossing pier

46 - Chiesa del Redentore: capital of a half-column and pilaster in one of the crossing piers

47 - Chiesa del Redentore: capital of a half-column and pilaster in one of the crossing piers

48 - Chiesa del Redentore: capital of a column of the exedra behind the main altar

49 - Chiesa del Redentore: capital of a column of the exedra behind the main altar

50 - Chiesa del Redentore: lower portion of the exedra columns, showing the entrance to the monks' choir

51 - Chiesa del Redentore: bases of the exedra columns

52 - Chiesa del Redentore: bases of the half-column of the entrance portal

53 - Chiesa del Redentore: bases of the half-columns in the nave

54 - Chiesa del Redentore: monks' choir

55 - Chiesa del Redentore: main altar

56 - GIROLAMO CAMPAGNA, bronze crucifix on the main altar

58 - Tommaso Ruer, *Christ Carrying the Cross.* Marble relief decorating the main altar

59 - GIROLAMO CAMPAGNA, *St. Mark.* Bronze statue on the left side of the main altar
60 - GIROLAMO CAMPAGNA, *St. Francis.* Bronze statue on the right side of the main altar

61 - Chiesa del Redentore: pavement of the presbytery

62 - Chiesa del Redentore: holy-water font at the left of the entrance

63 - Chiesa del Redentore: holy-water font at the right of the entrance

64 - FRANCESCO BASSANO, *The Nativity*. Altarpiece in the first chapel on the right

65 - CARLO and GABRIELE CALIARI, *The Baptism of Christ*. Altarpiece in the second chapel on the right

66 - School of JACOPO TINTORETTO, *The Flagellation*. Altarpiece in the third chapel on the right

67 - PALMA IL GIOVANE, *The Entombment*. Altarpiece in the third chapel on the left

68 - Francesco Bassano, *The Resurrection*. Altarpiece in the second chapel on the left
69 - Workshop of Jacopo Tintoretto, *The Ascension*. Altarpiece in the first chapel on the left
70 - Francesco Bassano, *The Resurrection* (detail). Altarpiece in the second chapel on the left

SURVEY REPORT

THE SURVEY WAS EXECUTED BY DR. ARCH. GILDA D'AGARO IN COLLA-BORATION WITH DR. ARCH. MARIA TARLÀ AND MARIO TOMASUTTI

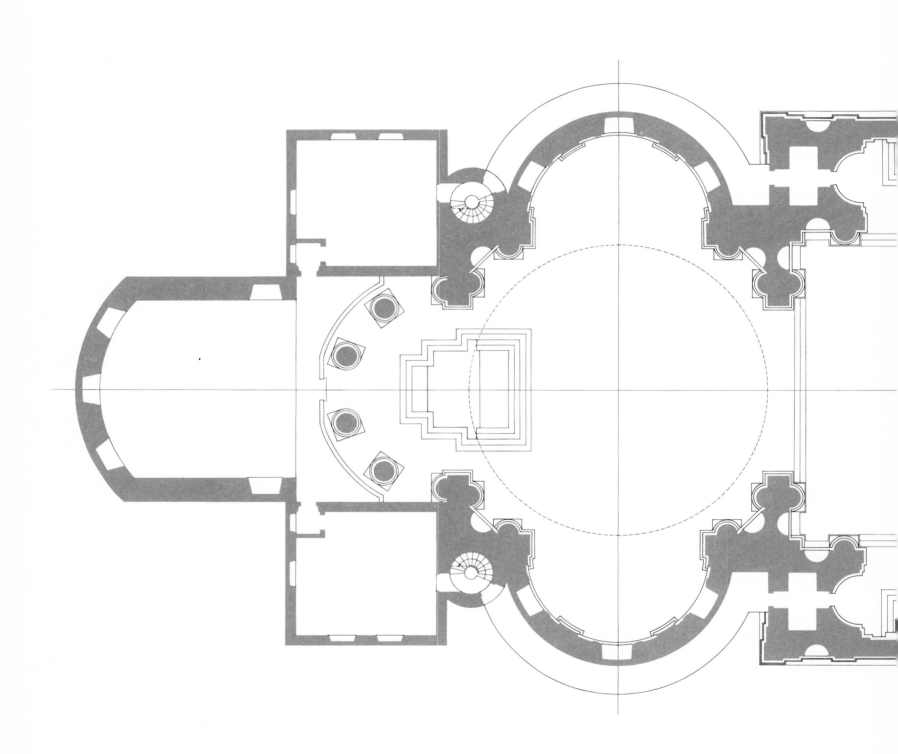

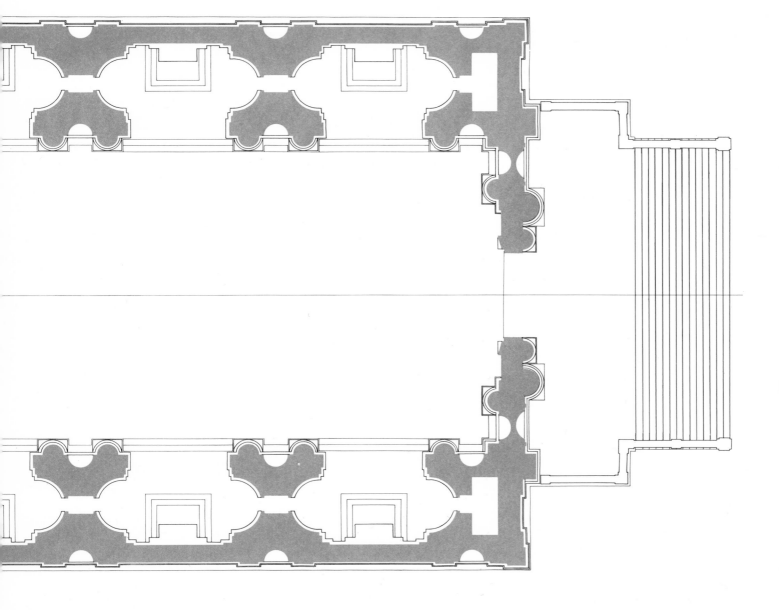

a - Chiesa del Redentore: plan

0 1 2 3 4 5   10   20m

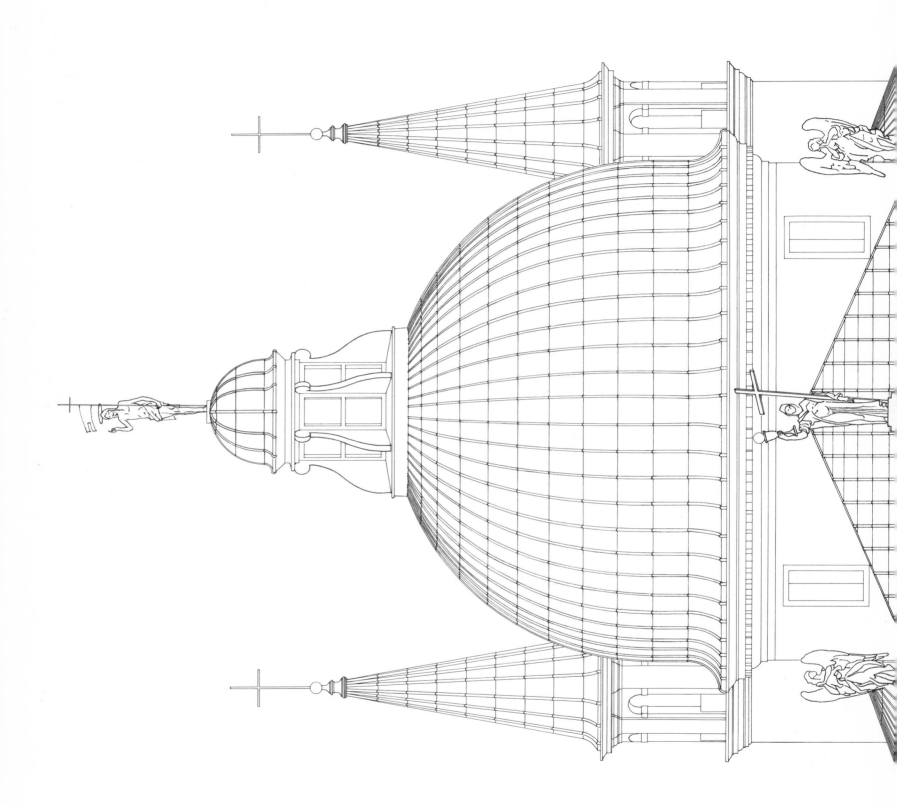

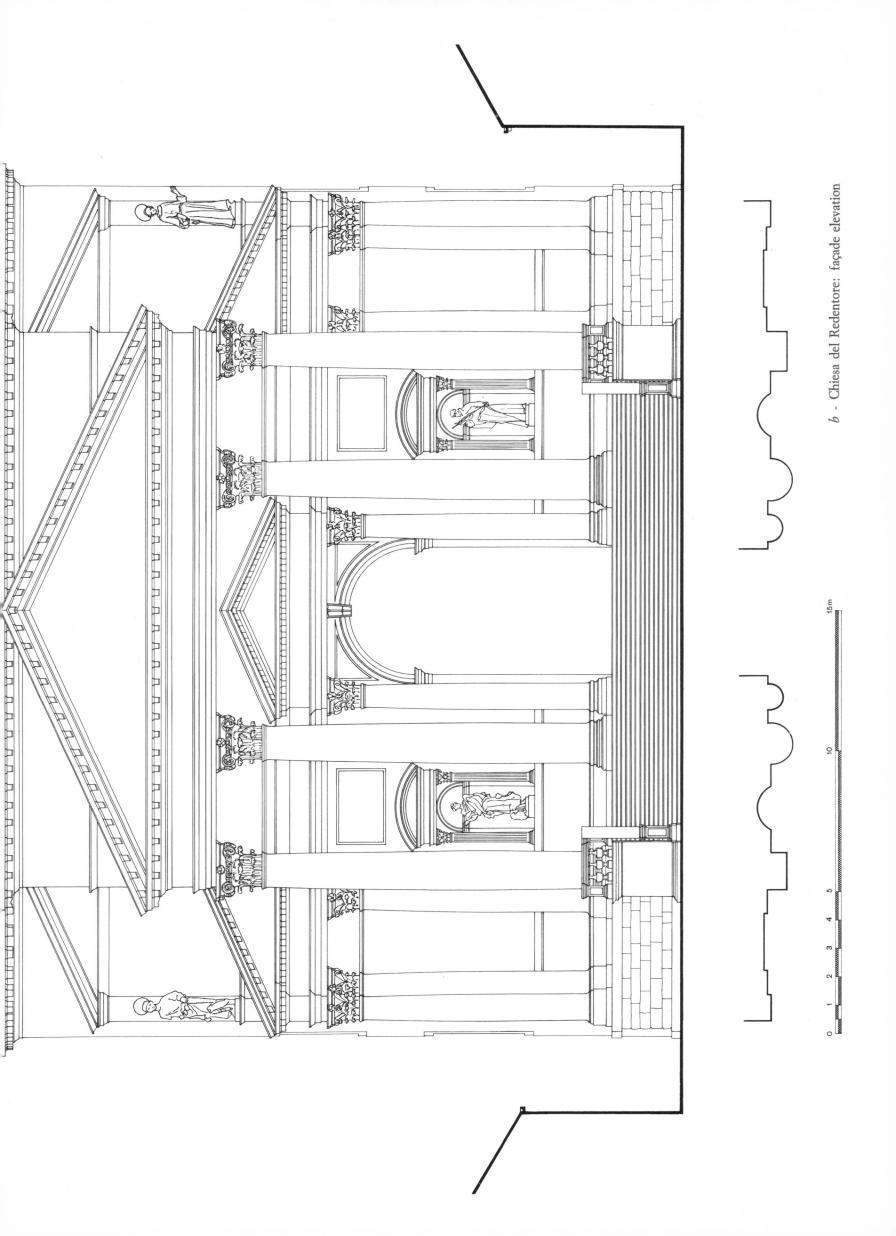

b - Chiesa del Redentore: façade elevation

0 1 2 3 4 5   10   20m

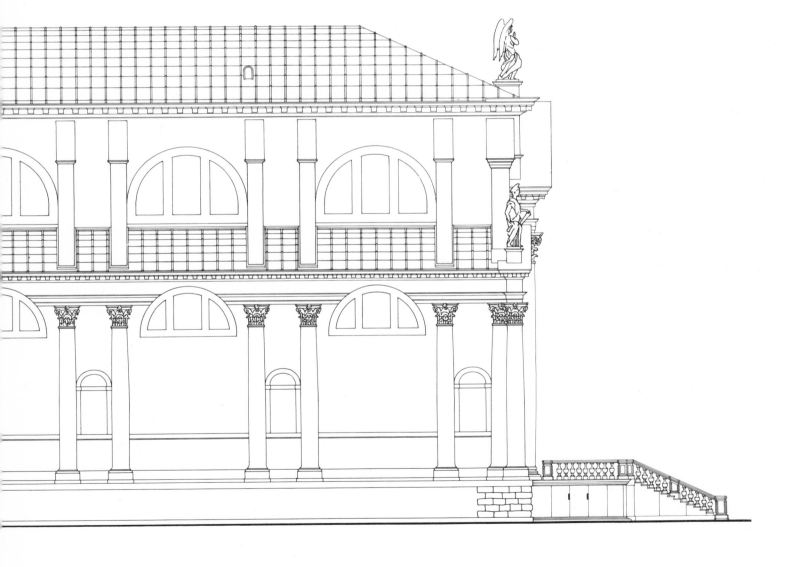

c - Chiesa del Redentore: side elevation

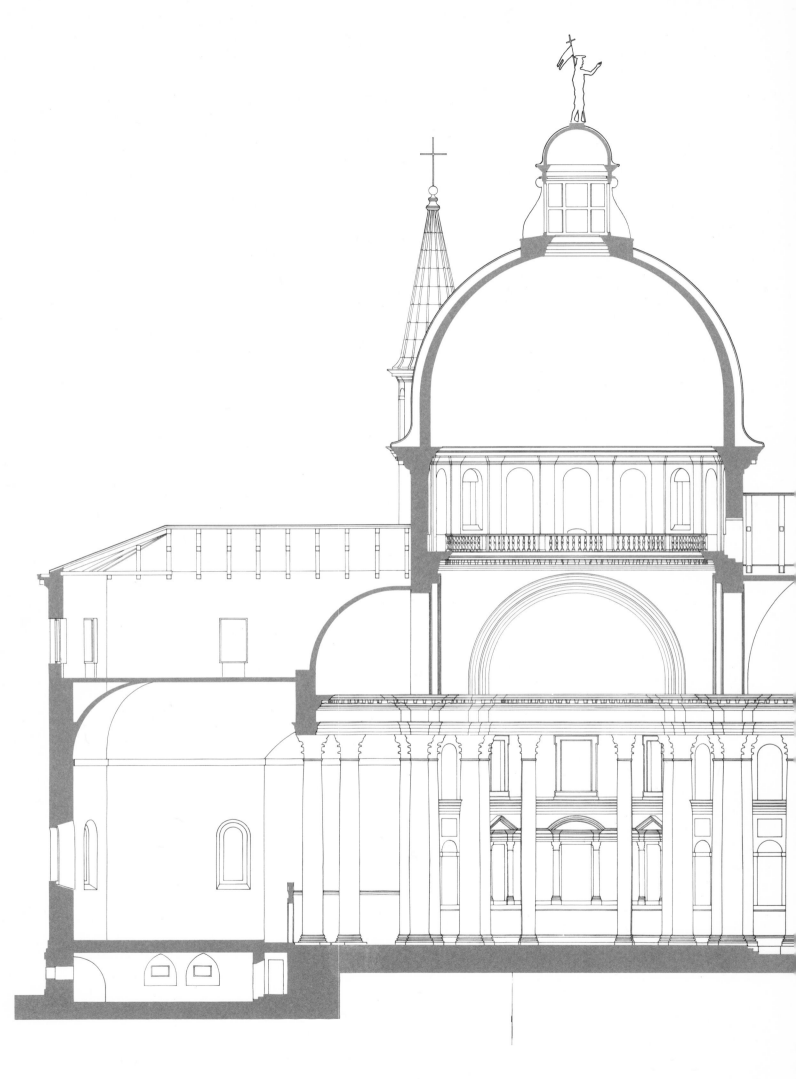

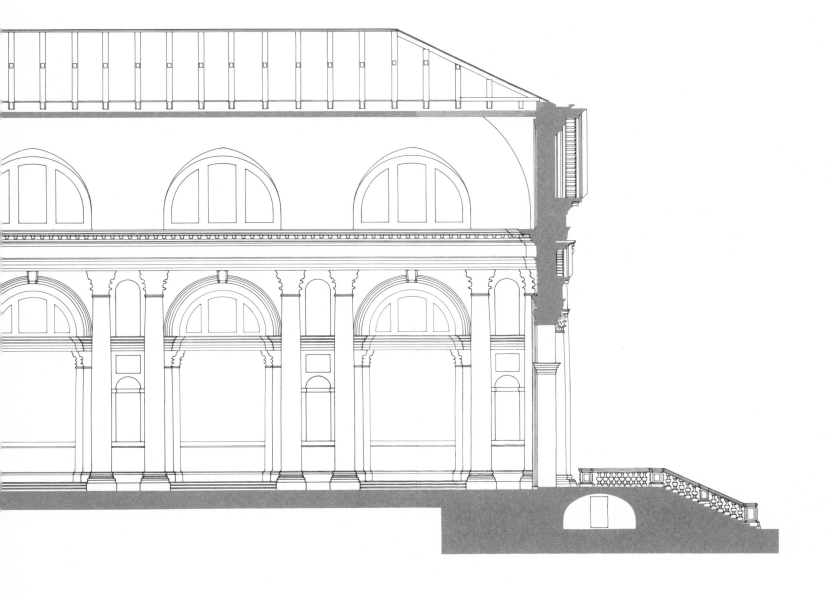

d - Chiesa del Redentore: longitudinal section

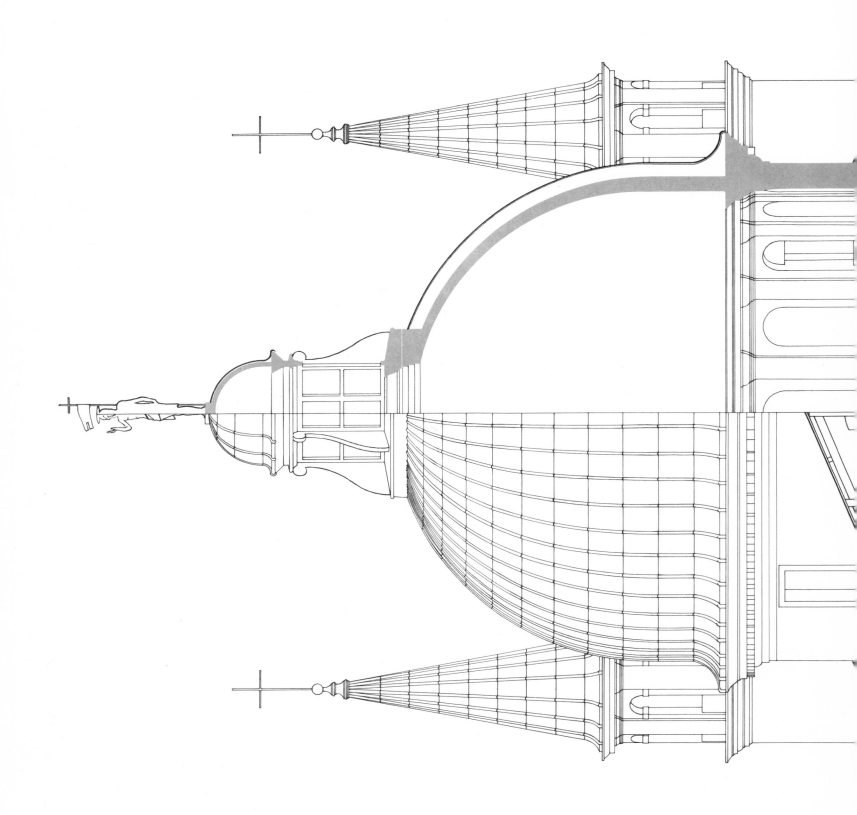

e - Chiesa del Redentore: transverse section showing nave and crossing

0 1 2 3 4 5 10 15m

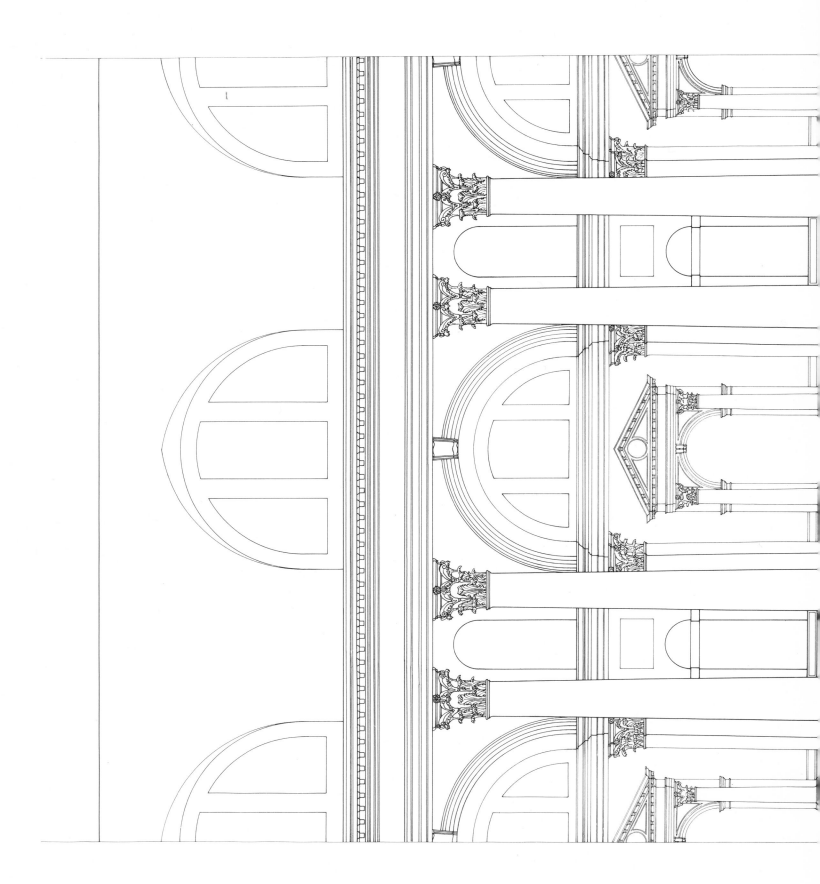

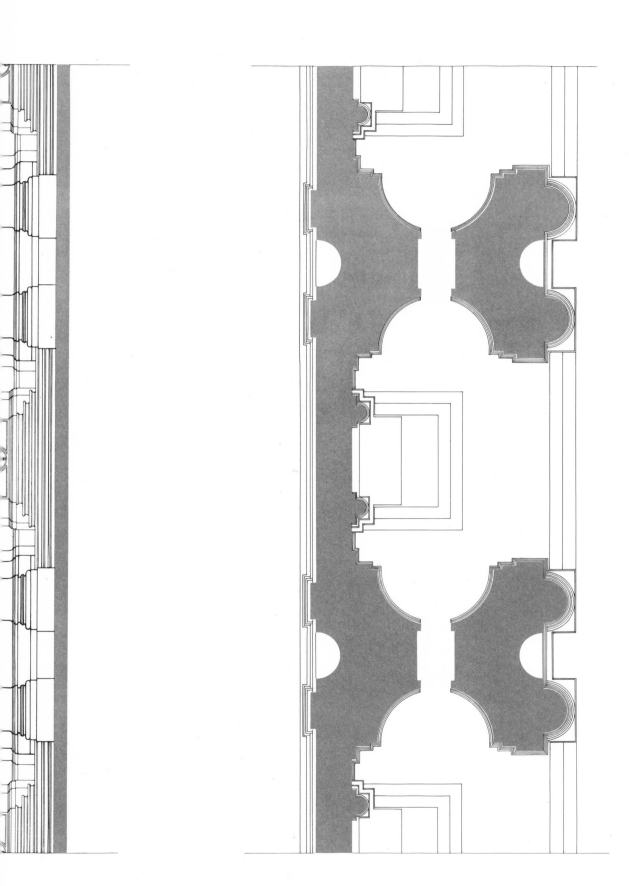

f - Chiesa del Redentore: elevation and plan of a portion of the nave

g - Chiesa del Redentore: elevation of a chapel

h - Chiesa del Redentore: section of a chapel

THIS MONOGRAPH ON THE CHIESA DEL REDENTORE WAS PRINTED IN VICENZA BY THE O.T.V. STOCCHIERO S.P.A, USING GARAMOND TYPE AND CARTA PAPERALBA FROM THE CARTIERA VENTURA FOR THE TEXT, CARTA RUSTICUS, ALSO FROM VENTURA, FOR THE SCALE DRAWINGS, AND CARTA LARIUS FROM THE CARTIERA BURGO FOR THE PLATES, THE PLATES WERE ALL PRINTED FROM BLOCKS BY A. MONTICELLI IN PADUA, AND THE SCALE DRAWINGS WERE PRINTED BY FOMERG IN PADUA. BINDING BY THE LEGATORIA EDITORIALE G. OLIVOTTO IN VICENZA.

PHOTO CREDITS: BORUI VENICE: 1; CINECOLORFOTO, VICENZA: XXIII; FIORENTINI, VENICE: 55; FONDAZIONE G. CINI, VENICE: 60; FOTOTECNICA, VICENZA: I-X, XIII, XVI; JOHN R. FREE-MAN & CO., LONDON: XXI, XXII; GABINETTO FOTOGRAFICO NAZIONALE, ROME: XI, XII, XIV, XV; MUSEO CORRER, VENICE: XVIII, XIX, XX; ROSSI, VENICE: a, b; 2-54, 56-59, 61-70; G. G. ZORZI, TRIESTE: XVII.